immersed in verse

Immersed in verse

An Informative, Slightly Irreverent & Totally Tremendous Guide to Living the Poet's Life

Allan Wolf

Illustrated by Tuesday Mourning

LARK BOOKS

A Division of Sterling Publishing Co., Inc.
New York / London

For Cheryl Bromley Jones

The Library of Congress has cataloged the hardcover edition as follows:
Wolf, Allan.
Immersed in verse : an informative, slightly irreverent & totally tremendous guide to living the poet's life / Allan Wolf.
p. cm.
Includes bibliographical references and index.
ISBN 1-57990-628-1
1. Poetry—Authorship. I. Title.
PN1059.A9W65 2006
808.1—dc22
2005024825

10 9 8 7 6 5 4 3 2 1

Published by Lark Books, A Division of
Sterling Publishing Co., Inc.
387 Park Avenue South, New York, N.Y. 10016

First Paperback Edition 2009
Text © 2006, Allan Wolf
Illustrations © 2006, Tuesday Mourning

Distributed in Canada by Sterling Publishing,
c/o Canadian Manda Group, 165 Dufferin Street
Toronto, Ontario, Canada M6K 3H6

Distributed in the United Kingdom by GMC Distribution Services,
Castle Place, 166 High Street, Lewes, East Sussex, England BN7 1XU

Distributed in Australia by Capricorn Link (Australia) Pty Ltd.,
P.O. Box 704, Windsor, NSW 2756 Australia

If you have questions or comments about this book, please contact:
Lark Books
67 Broadway
Asheville, NC 28801
(828) 253-0467

Manufactured in China

ISBN 13: 978-1-57990-628-3 (hardcover) 978-1-60059-510-3 (paperback)

For information about custom editions, special sales, and premium and corporate purchases, please contact Sterling Special Sales Department at 800-805-5489 or specialsales@sterlingpub.com.

Editor
JOE RHATIGAN

Art Director & Cover Designer
CELIA NARANJO

Illustrator
TUESDAY MOURNING

Art Assistant
BRADLEY NORRIS

Assistant Editor: Nathalie Mornu
Copy Editor: Carol Brunt
Proofreader: Karen Levy

Contents

Plunge into Words

Have you noticed how rhythm makes you move? How heavy bass vibrates the door panels of passing cars? Have you noticed the colors of a rainbow? How the stench of fireworks burns your eyes? How your cold winter hands sting under warm water? To be a poet is to notice. This book is about taking notice, then transforming what you notice into words.

Immersed in Verse is a cool plunge into poetry. In this book, you will find out what a poet is and what a poet does. You'll also explore all the things that poems can be and all the ways that poets write them. You'll take a look inside the poet's toolbox, which contains the basic tools that every poet needs. And you'll discover the Nine Habits of Highly Successful Poets. Included are tons of ideas for getting started writing your own poems, as well as ways to get your poems published.

But most important, you'll learn to see the world as a smorgasbord of poetic moments. Here's a sample. Take your pick.

rhyme verse common things poetry words journal rhyme empty tickle green mold g lyric tools o rhyme verse empty poetry time secret waffles on things poetry mold grows poetry empty of poetry

- In the kitchen's upper corner—dusty cobwebs hang like empty fishing nets.

- The grandfather cat: gray, lusterless fur draped over loosely assembled bones.

- At the empty feeder, three chickadees sing an empty feeder song.

- Your right elbow is in love with your left elbow, only your left elbow doesn't know.

- Under the blue couch, green mold grows wild on old pizza.

About the Poems in This Book

The poems I collected for this book come from lots of different poets. Some are famous, while others are friends of mine, kids I've taught over the years, and even teachers. The poems that don't have an author listed underneath them are mine.

Poems are all around us, waiting to be written. The world teems with words, images, ideas, sights, sounds, colors, anecdotes, notions, and emotions. Just as water is the stuff of life to a fish, the world is the stuff of life to a poet. All you need to do is dive in. *Immersed in Verse* will show you how to take the plunge.

Poetry & You

Poetry is the communication of something inside you: a thought, a story, a passion, an urge. In this section, I'll introduce some of the poetry basics, like what it means to be a poet, where poetry comes from, and a few secrets for poetic success. We are all born with a little bit of poetry inside us. A new-born's cry is that baby's first poetry recital. It might go something like this:

Waaaah! Waaaah!

Hic. Hic. Hic.

Waaaah! Waaaah!

Hic. Hic. Waaaah!*

*Translation

O! Harsh cold.

O! Sun-bright lights.

Rubber gloves upon my new-minted skin.

I am the lungfish emerging to gulp the air.

I am the peach pinched from the tree.

The innocent abducted by aliens.

Naked and misshapen

with only my voice to defend me.

Got milk?

Of Blooms & Booms & Secret Rooms

There are three essential elements of a poet's life: a bloom, a boom, and a secret room. The bloom is what catches the poet's eye. The boom is what explodes in the poet's mind. The secret room, with its magnificent views, exists in the poet's heart.

A Poet's Life

A poem can be a rocket—Zoom!—
that poets ride beyond the sky.

A poem can be a secret room
where poets watch the world walk by.

A poem can be loud fireworks—Boom!—
all whoosh and zing and sparkling fun.

A poem can be a quiet bloom
that turns its face to see the sun.

A poem can be a bloom, a boom,
a room, a zoom, a zing!

But poems are only flightless words
'til poets grant them wings.

It's better to live a poet's life
than live the life of kings and queens.

Blooms

Poems are everywhere. They lurk at your elbow, waiting for you to discover them. The poet's job is to spot them—to see them for what they are. The poet watches for poetic moments like a bee seeks out a bloom. In fact, the bee and the poet have a lot in common. The bee seeks out a bloom and transforms it into honey; the poet seeks out a moment and transforms it into a poem.

Booms

Author Barry Lane urges young writers to "explode the moment" in order to transform it into the stuff of poetry. No, he's not suggesting that poets should exchange their pencils for dynamite. This is Lane's way of urging poets to focus their attention on a single event (the bloom) and then expand on it in a detailed way (the boom). You might say that most poems are simply blooms transformed by booms. The result is always poetry.

Take a look at what happens when a bloom in a poet's eye becomes a boom in the poet's mind. The original bloom of my poem, titled "Hope," was the image of a frog I saw near a pond in Vermont. I exploded the moment by trying to imagine what the frog must have been feeling. I ought to mention that the frog was being chased by my eight-year-old son. To me, the frog seemed noble and full of hope as the small creature hopped from my son's hands toward the safety of the water. Hope? Hop? A poem had begun to grow. I observed the rhythm of the frog's hops. How could I give my poem the same rhythm? My poet's eye had observed the bloom. My poet's mind went boom! Here's the result.

Hope

Though its long leap

    is a great fete

there is much hope

    in a frog's hop:

will it land short

    on the pond shore?

or arrive home

    Ker PLOP?!

Secret Rooms

What, then, of the secret room? What, then, of the heart? The heart is where the magic really happens, after all. It was from my heart that I connected to the hopeful frog. Every poet's heart has a room with a view, an unobstructed view of the world. Some call it wisdom. Some call it intuition or empathy. I call it a room because it's a place that feels safe.

I call it a secret room, because no one can see it. It's something you feel inside. Call it whatever you want, but rest assured, if you're a poet, then you've got it. And that's good, because although the art of poetry can be taught, the heart of poetry cannot.

How about you? Do you want to be a poet? A poet with a bloom in your eye? A poet with a boom in your mind? A poet watching the world from a secret room held inside your heart? Well, then, let's start!

What Kind of Poet Are You?

I would like to introduce you now to the Stereotype Poets' Hall of Fame.

Classic Poet
Characteristics: swoony and pale
Usual Topics: nature, passion, love
Accessories: quill pen, puffy sleeves, notebook
Location: among the wild flowers

Beat Poet
Characteristics: way cool
Usual Topics: jazz, rebellion
Accessories: beret, bongos, notebook
Location: hip coffee shop

Angry Poet
Characteristics: paces back and forth, snarling and spitting
Usual Topics: why he is angry
Accessories: accessories make Angry Poet angry
Location: none of your business

Gothic Poet
Characteristics: stylishly apathetic
Usual Topics: death, darkness, death
Accessories: black clothing, eyeliner
Location: food court at the mall

Secret Poet
Characteristics: very...well...secretive
Usual Topics: That's a secret.
Accessories: notebook—actually, 12 notebooks
Location: at home

Hip-Hop Poet
Characteristics: compulsive rhyming
Usual Topics: politics, injustice, love
Accessories: saggy pants, notebook
Location: street corners, clubs, poetry slams

Professor Poet
Characteristics: rhyme-ophobic and cleverly obscure
Usual Topics: hard to tell
Accessories: podium, cardigan sweater, library card, laptop
Location: behind a cluttered desk

So what kind of poet are you?

Maybe you see a little bit of yourself in more than one member of the Stereotype Poets' Hall of Fame. The kind of poet you are may change from day to day. On Monday you may be Angry Poet. By Wednesday you're feeling a little bit like Secret Poet. But come Friday, Hip-Hop Poet emerges.

The truth is that most poets are not so easy to identify.

Do You Like Poetry? (A Guided Tour)

"Of course I do," you shout. "Why would I be reading this book if I didn't *like* poetry?"

To this I say with all my heart, "Waffles!"

Were I to ask, "Do you like *waffles*?" most everyone would answer "yes" without thinking. But now watch as I hold my poetic magnifying glass up in order to expose the waffle question completely:

Do you like waffles and everything that waffles mean? Do you like *eating* waffles? Do you like *making* waffles? Do you like cleaning up the batter bowl, the spoon, and the crusty waffle iron? And most important, what type of waffle do you like best? Blueberry, plain, chocolate chip? Do you like them with or without butter? And what about syrup? Boysenberry, strawberry, or maple? Powdered sugar? Applesauce? Fresh? Frozen? Square? Round?

Here's a question you rarely hear: "Do you like *music*?" The question you do hear is, "What *kind* of music do you like?" Well, it's the same with poetry. The important question is not "Do you like poetry?" The important question is "What *kind* of poetry do you like?" All at once, a world of answers opens up.

So what kind of poetry *do* you like? Take your pick:

Short Poems

Lines Written on the Antiquity of Microbes

Adam

had 'em.

—*Strickland Gillilan*

Long Poems

from Don Juan*

When Newton saw an apple fall, he found
In that slight startle from his contemplation—
'T is said (for I'll not answer above ground
For any sage's creed or calculation)—
A mode of proving that the earth turn'd round
In a most natural whirl called 'gravitation;'
And this is the sole mortal who could grapple,
Since Adam, with a fall or with an apple.

— *George Gordon, Lord Byron*

* This is only one of the 1,973 stanzas in *Don Juan*. The poem is a whopping 15,930 lines long!

Poems That Rhyme

from Sonnet 18

Shall I compare thee to a summer's day?
Thou art more lovely and more temperate:
Rough winds do shake the darling buds of May,
and Summer's lease hath all too short a date:

—William Shakespeare

Poems That Don't Rhyme

Rough

My life had gone
completely to the dogs
until the day I discovered
(to my astonishment)
that I was a dog myself.
Life was better after that.

Sad Poems

Poem

I loved my friend.
He went away from me.
There's nothing more to say.
The poem ends
Soft as it began—
I loved my friend.

—Langston Hughes

Funny Poems

I'm Thor!

The thunder god went for a ride
upon his favorite filly.
"I'm Thor," he cried.
And the horse replied,
"You forgot your thaddle, thilly!"

—Author unknown

Apology Poems

This Is Just To Say

I have eaten
the plums
that were in
the icebox

and which
you were probably
saving
for breakfast

Forgive me
they were delicious
so sweet
and so cold

—William Carlos Williams

Skateboard Poems

The Sidewalk Racer
or
On the Skateboard

Skimming
an asphalt sea
I swerve, I curve, I
sway; I speed to whirring
sound an inch above
the ground; I'm the sailor
and the sail, I'm the
driver and the wheel
I'm the one and only
single engine
human auto
mobile.

—Lillian Morrison

Poems That Teach

History Lesson

Higgledy Piggledy
William the Conqueror
Ousted King Harold in
Ten Sixty-six,
Sacked Anglo-Saxons and,
Normanmaniacal,
Cut off their heads and dis-
Played them on sticks.

Poems with No Punctuation

stars

in science today we learned
that stars are a mass of gasses that burned
out a long time ago only we don't know
that because we still see the glow

and i remembered my big brother donny
said he burned out a long time ago and i asked
him did that make him
a star

—Nikki Giovanni

Love Poems

from A Red, Red Rose

O, my luve is like a red, red rose,
That's newly sprung in June;
O, my luve is like a melodie
That's sweetly play'd in tune.

—Robert Burns

Quiet Poems

Shhhh

... poets
are in cahoots
with silence
but can't resist telling
how one teardrop
holds all the rain
you've ever heard,
sshhh ...

—Ray McNiece

Hate Poems

The Paragon

Yuk! How I hate Nancy Feder!
I can't think why the world would need her.
Since Nancy Feder moved next door,
life's not worth living anymore.
I don't know how my mother knows
she makes her bed and folds her clothes
and does her homework everyday
before she goes outside to play.
She's such a goodie, goodie, good
she'd make you barf! I bet she would!
(And you don't have to listen to
my mother rave the way I do!)
A rabbit's foot might bring me luck,
and then I'll see a moving truck.
Won't it be a sunny day,
when Nancy Feder moves away?

—Bobbi Katz

Loud Poems

from Big Noise Welcome Wagon

Big, broad, booming bass
Big heart-beats thumping by.
Taffy-pulled into Doppler sound
Melting down the heated streets.
Vibrations beat the metal walls.
Vibrate ricochet pinball falls
Vibrations beat each rattling pane
Like God's own urban timpani.
No trombones James Weldon J.
On this day God is Ooompah-Paaahing
On a Funkadelic TooooBaah!

Riddle Poems

Many eyes,
Never cries.

Answer: Potato

—*Anonymous*

A Riddle for All Seasons

In Spring she wears a new green hat.
In Summer she thinks that climbing is fun.
In Fall she resembles a calico cat.
In Winter she is a skeleton.

Answer: Tree.

Spanish Poems

El Coco

Compadre, cómpreme un coco.
Compadre, coco no compro,
que el que poco coco come,
poco coco compra.
Yo, como poco coco como
poco coco compro.

—*Traditional*

Poems That Smell

Politics

"I stink, but not as much as you,"
said the worn-out sock to the shabby shoe.
Said the shabby shoe to the worn-out sock,
"It's you who stink. Go take a walk!"
And so they walked on, left and right,
Until their stink was out of sight.

Barnes & Noble Booksellers #2614
2100 North Snelling Ave
Roseville, MN 55113
651-639-9256

STR:2614 REG:003 TRN:9150 CSHR:Kate S

EDUCATOR   EXP: 08/31/2011

Immersed in Verse: An In
  9781600595103
  (1 @ 12.95) Educator 20% (2.59)
  (1 @ 10.36)   10.36
Plants
  9781557996879
  (1 @ 12.99) Educator 20% (2.60)
  (1 @ 10.39)   10.39

Subtotal   20.75
Sales Tax (7.125%)   1.48
TOTAL   22.23
VISA DEBIT   22.23
  Card#: XXXXXXXXXXXXX4021

    Want to read your books on a dream
  vacation? Write a review at bn.com and
   be entered for a chance to win one!
   No purchase necessary. See official
   rules and details at bn.com/reviews.

V101.20   03/31/2010 01:17PM

CUSTOMER COPY

Poetry Poems

A Simile is Like a Song

A simile is like a song;
It's as easy to remember.
A metaphor makes soft white snow
Sifted sugar in December.
A little alliteration
Lets the lesson lilt and linger.
A rake that's been personified
Slips and hurts its finger.
Hyperbole exaggerates:
"Her crying caused a flood!"
Onomatopoeia imitates:
"KaBOOM! KerPLUNK! KaTHUD!"

—Author unknown

Fast Poems

Wednesday

Wake up and
rush run dash increase the
pace speed up go fast be
quick eat lunch and
hustle hurry hasten
race accelerate and quit.

Dialogue Poems

from Mother to Son

Well, son, I'll tell you:
Life for me ain't been no crystal stair.
It's had tacks in it,
And splinters,
And boards torn up,
And places with no carpet on the floor—
Bare.

—Langston Hughes

Poems, like waffles, are easy to limit in our minds. But by opening up the possibilities of what a poem can be, you discover a diverse buffet of verse to choose from.

So next time anyone asks, "Do you like poetry?" or even if someone asks that question's more accusatory form, "You don't really like poetry, do you?" just say, "Waffles."

A Poem for All Reasons

Why do you write poetry? Take this short quiz by answering either "true" or "false" to each statement.

I write poetry because it improves my grades.	T	F
I write poetry because it makes me popular.	T	F
I write poetry because my teacher makes me.	T	F
I write poetry because it helps me make sense of my world.	T	F
I write poetry because it gives me a feeling of satisfaction.	T	F
I write poetry because it calms me down and focuses my ideas and feelings.	T	F
I write poetry because I want to explain myself to other people.	T	F
I write poetry because it makes me better looking.	T	F

If you're like most poets, you answered "true" to more than one question. Ask a hundred poets why they write poetry and you'll get a hundred different answers. What's the one answer you probably *won't* get? "I write poems so kids can study them in English class and take tests on them."

Common to all poets is the desire to express their thoughts and feelings. The subject can be serious or whimsical, as shown in the two poems below. Both are *odes*, a poem in which the poet addresses a person, animal, object, or thing.

from Ode to a Nightingale

Thou wast not born for death, immortal Bird!
No hungry generations tread thee down;
The voice I hear this passing night was heard
In ancient days by emperor and clown;
Perhaps the self-same song that found a path
Through the sad heart of Ruth, when, sick for home,
She stood in tears amid the alien corn;
The same that ofttimes hath
Charm'd magic casements, opening on the foam
Of perilous seas, in faery lands forlorn.
—John Keats

from Ode to a Fetal Pig*

O fetal pig! O wond'rous swine
who gave your life to enrich mine.
To mourn your death would be to throw
away the gift that let me know
about the body so like mine,
O fetal pig, O wond'rous swine.

—*Yune Kyung Lee*

* Many biology classes include a lesson on dissecting a fetal pig.

John Keats hears the singing of a bird hidden in the trees, and he wants to lose himself in the bird's music. He reflects how generations of mortal poets have listened to the immortal song of the nightingale. Yune Kyung Lee's poem is more whimsical, and yet, like Keats, Lee goes beyond simple praise for her poem's subject. Through her humorous celebration of the fetal pig, Lee is able to comment seriously on the nature of sacrifice.

Inspiration is a fancy word that means an urgent need to express thoughts and feelings. Keats found inspiration sitting under a plum tree. Lee found inspiration sitting in biology class. To act on their inspiration, they each got out their poet toolbox and got to work.

I personally write poetry because I like to surprise myself. Many times my best ideas arise during the act of writing. To see what's beyond the next bend, an explorer must do a bit of hiking. Likewise, writers write their way from bend to bend, making discoveries along the way.

Writing poems won't make you better looking, but it *is* a great way to corral your scattered thoughts and thus allow yourself to create something that may bring you pleasure and peace of mind.

The Nine Habits of Highly Successful Poets

Habit #1:

Get Gonzo Over Words.

A painter loves her paints. A sculptor loves his clay. Skateboarders love their skateboards. And poets love their words. Try these three things:

Read.

Get a dictionary and use it. Make a mark in the margin next to each word you look up. You may end up with multiple marks next to the same word. You live. You learn. You forget. You learn again.

Carry a notebook and pen with you at all times to write down any good words you come across, scenes you experience, or images you see. Become a collector of words, phrases, sayings, clever ideas, and verbal pictures.

Habit #2:

Don't Be a Naked Fashion Designer.

Poetry is a lot like sports. There's more to being a well-rounded athlete than simply playing the game. To play it better, you might do some weight training. You'd study the plays and the strategies. You'd work on your techniques, and maybe even subscribe to a magazine that focuses on your sport. It's the same with poetry.

Just writing poetry is fine, but if you don't take an interest in poetry in general, then you're in danger of getting stuck on one of the low rungs of the poetry ladder. The more you learn about poetry, the more you memorize poetry, the more you experience poetry, the higher up the poetry ladder you'll climb.

You can simply write poetry, if you wish. Many people do, and they do just fine. But writing poetry without experiencing all the poetry around you is a bit like being a fashion designer who doesn't wear clothes. The act of writing is only part of the overall process of poetry. Begin to balance your writing with other poetry experiences. Get to know poetry. Read it. Go to a poetry reading or two. Talk to poetry lovers about poetry.

Habit #3:

Live Life as If Only Two Things Matter.

You:

Enter into a relationship with your Self. We are all works in progress. Be sure to reflect on who you are. Don't become complacent. Socrates said the unexamined life is not worth living, but I really think author Geneen Roth put it best when she said that awareness is learning to keep yourself company. Choosing to spend an evening at home reading a book or working on a poem will not make you an instant geek. Of course, if you are a geek, then by all means, embrace your geekiness. Write your own geek manifesto! Whoever you are, get to know yourself.

The World:

Enter into a relationship with the world. Read the newspaper. Find out what's going on, and do your best to form an opinion about it. Get out of the house and get involved, live life, and then take out your pen and get writing! There is no such thing as a bored poet.

Habit #4:

Eat Your Words!

Make sure that your reading diet is well balanced. Little chocolate doughnuts may be an essential part of my personal diet, but I always add variety—potato chips, beef jerky, goldfish crackers. It's the same with reading. Most of us live within easy reach of an all-you-can-eat buffet of words. Newspapers, novels, nonfiction, *Teen People*, X-Men comics, cereal boxes, and, of course, poetry of all sorts.

Habit #5:

Do More. Watch Less.

Know the difference between doing and watching. Unlike watching, doing resonates in your soul, sticks to your ribs, and satisfies you longer once you're done doing it. Just be sure to balance your doing and your watching in healthy proportions.

Habit #6:

Realize That Poetry Ain't Always Pretty.

Show me a picturesque pond with regal swimming swans, and I'll show you a muddy bank full of swan poop. Without ugly, there would be no beautiful. Likewise, the subjects of your poetry need not be huge and important (divorce, death, world hunger). Don't forget that there are worlds of wonder within a robin's egg, a cast-off shoe, or the contents of your pockets. So train yourself to be a hunter of the small and insignificant. And while you're observing the "good," don't forget the "bad" and the "ugly." They come as a set. The rainbow and the rain go hand in hand. The mighty oak was once an acorn. Note the grace of the swan on the water as well as the trace of the swan on the land—the poop.

Habit #7:

Learn to Love Your Gorilla Words.

I guarantee that nearly every professional writer has looked back at his or her first draft and winced in pain. "Ugghh! Did I write that? I must have been writing in my sleep! It looks like a four-year-old wrote that—a four-year-old gorilla—a stupid four-year-old gorilla who is one banana shy of a bunch." In fact I said it myself—just now.

The point is that's how it's done. You need to get the gorilla words down first. Most "writer's block" is created by unreasonable expectations. If you sit down and decide that you're going to write an award-winning, perfect, awesome poem, you'll likely fail. Writers who approach the blank page (or computer screen) this way are being unfair to themselves as well as to their poor unborn poems. Don't be afraid to generate a lot of gorilla words on your way to creating a top-banana poem. So write a little bit at a time. Take baby steps. Two lines here. Two lines there. And don't concern yourself with the quality of these early attempts.

Habit #8:

Write Every Day.

I'm not saying you need to squander the ever-fleeting moments of your youth hunkered over your desk, ruining your eyes, and developing a callused, leathery bump on your finger. But write every day. Even just a little. Even just a couple of words. Find a good sturdy notebook and set yourself a reasonable goal: two sentences every day. Be sure to date each entry. It doesn't matter what you write. You're more than welcome to write *more* than two lines, but you're not allowed to write fewer than two.

"But what will I write about?" you cry. Write about your day. You don't have to get deep (although you can). The object is to write automatically. It's enough simply to jot down an outline of how you passed your day. After a month, you'll be surprised by how much life there is in a simple accounting of your normal routines. Your journal will become an honest and beautiful display of boring little miracles. You'll also begin to understand that your writing and your life are works in progress.

Habit #9:

Play!

Unlike your food, words are perfectly okay to play with. Spell them wrong on purpose. Turn them upside down. Read them backward. Rhyme, don't rhyme, repeat. It's good to know the rules. Why? Because it's fun to break them. Whether the poems you like to write are serious, playful, mournful, or silly, playing and experimenting with your words will help fill your poem with life and vitality.

Take the Daily Writing Pledge

Having trouble getting the words down? Forgetting your two sentences every day? Write the pledge below in the front of your journal.

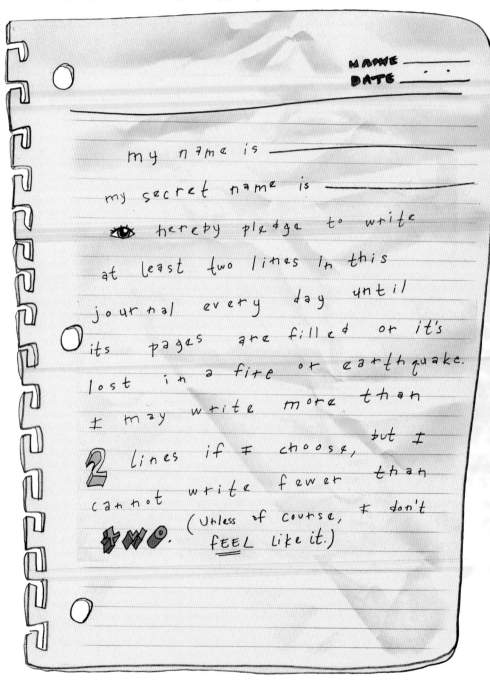

NAME _____
DATE _____

my name is _____

my secret name is _____

👁 hereby pledge to write

at least two lines in this

journal every day until

its pages are filled or it's

lost in a fire or earthquake.

I may write more than

2 lines if I choose, but I

cannot write fewer than

TWO. (Unless of course, I don't

FEEL like it.)

I give myself permission
to write absolutely anything.
It doesn't have to be nice.
It doesn't have to be funny.
Of course, if it happens to be
all of these things that's just
fine. But the absolute only
thing that my daily entries
must be is ~~the~~ two or
more lines long (not counting
the date).

Given by my hand on this _____
day of _____ in the year _____.

Your Poetry Toolbox

Every craft has its tools and rules. All carpenters need equipment (a hammer, a saw) and they need a few rules ("Measure twice, cut once." "Watch out for your fingers."). Poets are no different. This section of the book will give you a glimpse into the poet's toolbox, which contains the nuts and bolts of the poet's craft. You'll learn to identify, by name, the basic parts of a poem. I'll give you some strategies for reading a poem, and, of course, I'll define some of a poetry writer's typical instruments, devices, and strategies.

How to (a-hem) Read a Poem

You may have been taught to read poems as if you're a detective approaching the scene of a crime. The poem is protected by yellow and black barricade tape. You flash your badge (to some low ranking uniformed officer). You duck under the tape and start looking for evidence: a body, a weapon, a suspect, a witness, a motive. Catch the criminal and you win!

But a poem is not a whodunit mystery. In fact, a poem may actually ask more questions than it answers. Despite what you may have been told in school, poems are not meant to be "solved"; they are meant to be savored. Here are some tips for reading and enjoying poetry:

- Don't worry if parts of the poem leave you bewildered. Remember that poets are sometimes attempting to put into words what can't be said, which can result in some pretty perplexing poems.

- Be sure to "read" the poem's images—the pictures that emerge from the words. Hold these pictures in your mind's eye. Let them linger there.

- Slow doooown. Read the poem more than once. Read it out loud.

- At some point, look up any words you don't understand (but do this *after* reading the poem straight through for the first time).

- Notice any poetic devices you like or sounds and rhythms that grab your attention.

- Look at how words are placed on the page and how punctuation and line breaks are used.

- Try writing down the lines that evoke strong emotions in you. Or write down lines that confuse you.

Toys of the Trade

You don't need much in the way of tools (or toys) to get started writing poetry. A pen, some paper, the whole world around you ... That's about it. Poetry is about as low-maintenance as it gets, but here's some advice on the few things you will need:

Pens

If you're the type of person who can keep track of a favorite pen for months, then by all means buy yourself an expensive pen with a golden nib. If you're like me and misplace five or six pens a day, it's best not to become emotionally involved with each fly-by-night writing tool. I prefer medium-point, disposable pens with black ink. But anything will do.

I have a habit of carrying a pen tucked behind my right ear (my left ear is more sticky-outty, so it has no gripping power), so I like a lightweight pen that won't bend my ear or clatter to the floor when I stoop to tie my shoe.

Pen caps are important to me, too, because I usually have a pen in my pants pocket. If the pen in your pocket has no cap, you're in danger of ink hemorrhage—when, without warning, your pen silently explodes in your pocket, leaving an ink stain the size of a half-dollar on what may be the only pair of pants you look good in.

If you look good in all your pants, then don't worry about the pen cap. For the rest of us, it's not worth the risk.

What about pencils, you ask? Whatever floats your boat, I say. I don't care for them myself. Ink is easier to read. Ink doesn't smudge when you sweat on it. Ink can survive a chocolate milk spill. It's best not to be too picky. If you squander every minute of your precious writing time looking for the perfect pen, then what you really need is therapy. So grab whatever you've got and start writing!

The Bent Book

The well-prepared poet always has a notepad on hand. I recommend something small, such as a 3 x 5-inch spiral-bound model that can easily fit in your back pocket. Those of you who carry your notebook in this manner will notice the way in which it bends itself into the perfect curve of your rear end, hence the name *bent book*.

Why carry a notepad? Just think of your world as a big supermarket. Now think of yourself as a customer in a supermarket and your notepad as the shopping cart. Every day we walk down the aisles of life: health and beauty, fresh produce, frozen foods, the candy section. As we walk, we gather the ingredients we need to prepare a feast of words.

So as you walk through the aisles of *your* life, see what the shelves hold—images, sounds, smells, characters, mannerisms, funny names, striking metaphors, details, descriptions, and dialogue. You don't even need a shopping list. Just reach out for whatever catches your eye and add it to your cart. Once you're back home and sitting down to write, you can unpack those grocery bags, look over the results of your shopping spree, and start cooking up a poetry stew.

HOMEMADE BENT BOOK

Make your own traveling journal. This book is great because you can roll it up and keep it almost anywhere. Don't worry; the sewing is easy to do.

WHAT YOU NEED

- 1 piece of cardboard
  (5 x 10 inches)
- 10 to 12 sheets of paper
  (each $4^1/2$ x 9 inches)
- Nail
- Heavy thread
- Sewing needle
- Scissors

WHAT YOU DO

1. Place the cardboard on a table with a short end facing you. Roll it up, and then unroll it. The cardboard should stay sort of bent.

2. Fold the cardboard in half. Then fold the sheets of paper in half and place them inside the cardboard cover. This is what your book will end up looking like.

3. Unfold the book. With the nail, poke three holes through the fold in the book. Make each hole about 1 inch apart. Wiggle the nail to make the holes big enough so the needle will fit through.

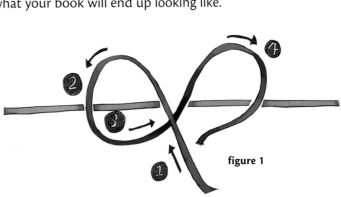

figure 1

4. Thread the needle, and sew up the book, following figure 1. As you insert the needle through the center hole from the outside of the book, make sure you leave a tail on the outside. When you're done, tie a double knot and trim the ends of the thread.

5. Experiment with different sizes, and try adding more pages if you like.

Diaries Are for Sissies

At least that's what many people think. *Not true.* Lewis and Clark, the great explorers, both kept diaries, and *they* certainly weren't sissies. That's because Lewis and Clark each called his diary a *journal.* So call it a journal. Call it a diary. Call it a banana if you like. Whatever you call it, get one and write in it—not just poetry, but whatever you can think of. Remember Habit #8 on page 25: write a little every day if you can. Experiment with different notebooks until you have one that's just right for you. Maybe you want one with no lines in it. Or how about a three-ring binder? It's up to you. (For more on journals, see page 68.)

Computer

The bent book and trusty pen are really all the equipment you'll need while you're "in the field." But once indoors, you'll typically want to type your handwritten words into a computer. This will allow you to play with the shape and order of your words and juggle them into the form you choose. Once you've got everything just how you want it, you can print out your writing, which gives you a chance to see it in a whole new light. For some reason, it's easier to revise a poem once it's typed up neatly.

Laptops are wonderful because you can take them on your poetry adventures. They're still not as convenient as the low-tech bent book and pen, but they're pretty nifty nonetheless.

Poetic Devices

Okay. You observed. You experienced. You wrote. Now what? How do you turn those random observations into poetry? Luckily, your poet toolbox contains a range of top-of-the-line *poetic devices*—tricks of the trade that turn your ideas into writing and your writing into poems. These are the poet's power tools, the techniques that can transform the ordinary into the extraordinary. Here are a few all-time favorite poetic devices.

Metaphors Be with You

"Why don't poets just say what they mean?" Ever since schools began making poetry the object of tests, frustrated students have asked this question. To this time-weary battle cry I answer this: why do stained-glass windows always block the sun with all those annoying colors and patterns? Many times poets don't "just say what they mean" because they are attempting to say what can't be said.

Really good poems allow the reader to feel something new or see an ordinary thing in an extraordinary way. Good poems make connections in the reader's mind until the reader says, "Ah, ha!" Sometimes, a good poem provides an answer to a question. But just as often, a poem *asks* a question with no clear answer.

When it comes to saying what can't be said, the poet's best friends are similes and metaphors. Poet or not, most everyone is familiar with metaphor and simile, probably because teachers find this poetic pair easy to teach. Students find them easy to spot on a test. And poets find them easy to write.

Metaphorical language compares two seemingly unlike things in order to point out a similarity. You may never have considered fog to have much in common with a cat. Yet Carl Sandburg points out the similar way they both move. Readers combine the two ideas (cat + fog), conjure their own pictures, and say, "Ah ha, I see what you mean!" The poet simply suggests the comparison. It is the readers who conjure up their own personal images to watch the comparison at work. This is how metaphors create a collaboration between poet and reader.

> **Fog**
> **The fog comes**
> **on little cat feet.**
>
> **It sits looking**
> **over harbor and city**
> **on silent haunches**
> **and then moves on.**
> —*Carl Sandburg*

So what's the difference between metaphors and similes? Technically, simile is a *type* of metaphor. You can distinguish simile from metaphor by looking for the telltale "like" or "as." But that's not really the point. Both simile and metaphor focus on the similarities between seemingly different things. Poets use simile to *tell* us the similarity exists, while metaphor *shows* the similarity. In the second stanza, Sandburg does not tell us the fog is *like* a cat; instead, he *shows* us the fog moving in a catlike way.

Here are a few well-known metaphors and similes. Notice how the comparisons are not always spelled out, as in "The early bird catches the worm."

Examples of Metaphors

The early bird catches the worm.

It'll be a piece of cake.

"The moon was a ghostly galleon tossed upon cloudy seas." (Alfred Noyes)

"The moon's the North Wind's Cookie."
(Eve Merriam)

My teacher erupted in anger.

Her eyes burned a hole right through me.

Examples of Similes

You are as smart as a whip.

He is as light as a feather.

The night was "like a patient etherized upon a table." (T.S. Elliott)

Life is like a box of chocolates.

She's as mean as a junkyard dog.

Metaphors don't have to be confined to a short line or two. Sometimes, poets explore a single metaphor over the course of an entire poem. This is known as an *extended metaphor.*

Personification

Personification means to give human qualities to nonhuman things. Personification is magical, a kind of poetic wizardry. With a wave of the pen, poets can make clouds weep, brooks babble, and birds sing out hello.

Examples of Personification

The sun hides its face.

The broom waits patiently in the corner.

"Night woke to blush." (Langston Hughes)

The spider bowed her welcome to the fly.

The tree's branches kissed the ground.

"Oh, happy dagger." (William Shakespeare)

Repetition, Repetition, Repetition

Poets repeat words, phrases, and entire lines to establish a predictable rhythm that draws the reader into the poem's groove.

from O Christmas Tree

O Christmas tree, O Christmas tree,
Thy leaves are so unchanging;
O Christmas tree, O Christmas tree,
Thy leaves are so unchanging.
—*Author unknown*

from Ring Out, Wild Bells

Ring out the old, ring in the new,
Ring, happy bells, across the snow:
The year is going, let him go;
Ring out the false, ring in the true.
—*Alfred, Lord Tennyson*

from Out of the Cradle Endlessly Rocking

Out of the cradle endlessly rocking,
Out of the mocking-bird's throat, the musical shuttle,
Out of the Ninth-month midnight.

—*Walt Whitman*

from The Bells

How it swells!
How it dwells
On the Future! — how it tells
Of the rapture that impels
To the swinging and the ringing
Of the bells, bells, bells —
Of the bells, bells, bells, bells,
Bells, bells, bells —
To the rhyming and the chiming of the bells!

—*Edgar Allan Poe*

Onomatopoeia

This one is self-explanatory. Words that sound like the things they mean are cool! Mud would be no fun without "squish." Potato chips would be boring without "crunch." Imagine trying to dive without "splash," or run a stick across a picket fence without "clatter."

Talk

Squawk. Clank.
Crash. Boing.
Drip. Buzz.
Tick. Tock.

Bird. Chain.
Glass. Spring.
Drop. Fly.
Clock talk.

Beat, Meter, and Rhythm

Every song has a groove, an essential rhythm that the music could not live without. Poems are no different. The best way to learn poetry's rhythm is to read it a lot and say it out loud.

A poem's special groove is really the result of poetry's dream team: beat, meter, and rhythm. I'll illustrate this using the first few lines of Edward Lear's rhythm-rich adventure poem titled "The Jumblies":

> **They went to sea in a Sieve, they did,**
> **In a Sieve they went to sea:**
> **In spite of all their friends could say,**
> **On a winter's morn, on a stormy day,**
> **In a Sieve they went to sea!**

The poem's beat is easy to feel, like the bass drum of a marching band:

> **they WENT to SEA in a SIEVE they DID**
> **in a SIEVE they WENT to SEA.**

What most people call a *beat* is called a *foot* in poetry lingo. Each foot is made up of some combination of stressed and unstressed syllables. The first line of "The Jumblies" consists of four feet: *they went; to sea; in a Sieve;* and *they did.*

A poem's *meter* tells us the number of beats (or feet) in each line. The first line has four beats (*tetrameter*). The second line has three beats (*trimeter*). The poem's rhythm is created by the flow of syllables across the steady structure established by the meter and the beats.

A Foot by Any Other Name

Just like the human foot, the poetic foot comes in many shapes and sizes. It's what makes a poem dance. A metrical foot is a unit of measure based on the combination of stressed and unstressed syllables. Even a poem with the same number of feet in each line can combine a variety of foot sizes across the poem's steady beat. The type of foot used and the number of feet per line create a poem's rhythm. So, it's up to you. Will your poem waltz, tango, or cha cha cha?

Foot Name	Syllable	Sound Example(s)
Iamb	tee TUM	because, in love, enough, they went
Trochee	TUM tee	novel, basket, stop it, highway
Anapest	tee tee TUM	disregard, by myself, in a sieve
Dactyl	TUM tee tee	Emily, riveted, kiddy swing
Spondee	TUM TUM	green truck, white hot, best man
Pyrrhic*	tee tee	for the, in a

*A pyrrhic foot is usually followed by a spondee, thus creating a unit of two feet (tee tee TUM TUM) as in *for the best man* or *in a green truck*. This two-foot variation is sometimes called a *double iamb*.

Rhyme Doesn't Pay...Or Does It?

Pick up almost any book of "grown-up" poetry written today and you'll notice that the poems rarely rhyme. What's *with* that?

Rhyme is likely the most ancient and most important of all the poet's tools. Poets have been using rhyme since the beginning of, well, time. Yet many of today's most critically acclaimed poets leave rhyme at the bottom of their toolbox, untouched—like the slightly-out-of-style sweater you never take out of your drawer.

Personally, I like rhyme, although I admit that I use it mostly when I'm writing for young kids, when I'm writing lyrics to a song, or when my goal is humor. Maybe I shy away from rhyme because I find it very hard to do well. Rhyme is dangerous, and, like any potentially lethal substance, should be used sparingly and handled gently.

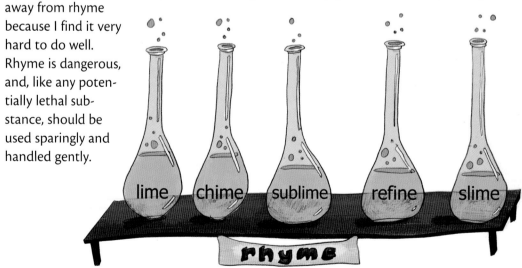

lime chime sublime refine slime

rhyme

Rhymes can be serious:

from Upon Julia's Clothes

Whenas in silks my Julia goes,
Then, then, methinks, how sweetly flows
That liquefaction of her clothes.
—*Robert Herrick*

Rhymes can be silly:

from A Sad Tale or Hey, Who Stole My Seat?

Without my behind, I am in quite a muddle.
I'll have to have surgeons perform a re-buttal!

Rhymes can be adventurous:

from Paul Revere's Ride

Listen, my children, and you shall hear
Of the midnight ride of Paul Revere,
On the eighteenth of April, in Seventy-Five;
Hardly a man is now alive
Who remembers that famous day and year.
—*Henry Wadsworth Longfellow*

To a poet, rhyme is a powerful tool that can potentially detract from the poem's overall effect. I'm not saying that poems should *never* rhyme, just that they shouldn't rhyme all the—er—time. Rhyme should never be an end in itself, but only one of a long list of potential ingredients the poet might use to flavor the pot.

Writing unrhymed verse allows poets to focus on meaning. If the subject of your poem is an orange, for example, you could spend days looking for a word that rhymes with orange only to come up with "door hinge." Then you have to figure out what a door hinge has to do with an orange, and suddenly you're thinking about door hinges instead of oranges.

I have already confessed that I write poems that rhyme. I'll even confess that I own a—gasp!—rhyming dictionary. But let me close with this last bit of advice when you're forced to decide "to rhyme or *not to* rhyme?" Don't use the word that rhymes; use the word that's right.

Internal Rhyme

We're used to finding rhyming words at the end of a poetic line (called *external rhyme*). Long ago, when poems were always spoken aloud, rhymes would indicate to listeners where one line ended and the next one began. But rhyme can happen anywhere within a poem. *Internal rhymes* (sometimes called *medial rhymes*) are rhymes that occur at the beginning or in the middle of a poetic line. Read these two examples out loud and listen for the difference in overall rhythm and effect. The rhyming words have been highlighted so you can visually follow the different rhyming patterns.

External Rhyme

Heart

Your heart's no bigger then your *fist.*
It falls in love when you've been *kissed.*
I take that back. That's just a *myth.*
Ask any cardiolo*gist.*

Internal Rhyme

Hearts

The *first burst* **when egg becomes child,**
our *hearts start* **the** *show.*
Slow **and steady when we** *sleep.*
Keep **the** *beat,* **the** *meter***—steady** *rocks.*
Clocks, **they tick and** *tock* **to track the time.**
And when two lovers *meet***—they chime.**

Notice how some of the internal rhymes above connect the last word of a line to the first word of the line that follows (show/slow, sleep/keep, rocks/clocks). The words "beat" and "meter" are even echoed two lines later in the word "meet." Internal rhyme can intensify a poem's rhythm, which is why it is often found in hip-hop and rap lyrics.

Other Examples of Internal Rhyme

There are strange things *done* **in the midnight** *sun*
by the men who moil for gold.
　　　—Robert Service

Sister, my sister, O *fleet sweet* **swallow.**
　　　— Algernon Charles Swinburne

... and *croon* **their** *blues* **to an** *amused moon...*
　　　—Patricia Smith

Anatomy of a Poem

TITLE

Where I'm From

REPETITION
The phrase "I am from" guides the reader from beginning to end.

I am from clothespins,
from Clorox and carbon-tetrachloride,
I am from the dirt under the back porch.
(Black, glistening,
it tasted like beets.)
I am from the forsythia bush
the Dutch elm
whose long-gone limbs I remember
as if they were my own.

PROPER NAMES
Clorox, carbon tetra-chloride, forsythia, and Dutch elm.

VIVID IMAGES
that rely on the senses. taste of beets, sound of yelling, smell of coffee.

I'm from fudge and eyeglasses,
from Imogene and Alafair.
I'm from the know-it-alls
and the pass-it-ons,
from Perk up! and Pipe down!
I'm from He restoreth my soul
with a cottonball lamb
and ten verses I can say myself.

SPECIFIC DETAIL
Fudge, Clorox, "Perk up! and Pipe down!"

VARIATION on "I am from" phrase varies the rhythm.

I'm from Artemus and Billie's Branch,
fried corn and strong coffee.
From the finger my grandfather lost
to the auger,
the eye my father shut to keep his sight.

MUSIC created with alliteration (assonance and consonance). "finger my grand-father lost to the auger."

Under my bed was a dress box
spilling old pictures,
a sift of lost faces
to drift beneath my dreams.
I am from those moments—
snapped before I budded—
leaf-fall from the family tree.
—*George Ella Lyon*

STANZA BREAKS
Divide poem into independent stanzas.

Poem has a sense of **CONCLUSION.**

STRONG WORDS ALONG THE RIGHT MARGIN. box, pic-tures, faces, dreams, moments, etc.

41

What makes "Where I'm From" a poem?

The Unexpected: Lyon does the unexpected by substituting "a place" with a series of sensory images and details. We typically think of ourselves as being from a *location*, not from objects (clothespins), from sayings (perk up and pipe down), or from food (fried corn and strong coffee).

Images: The poem is a montage of images that create a sensory experience no linear narrative could hope to match.

Repetition and Variation: Lyon repeats the phrase "I am from" so it becomes a steady part of the poem's overall rhythm and feel. Lyon also varies the phrase to "I'm from" and, simply, "from," which helps the poem avoid redundancy and quickens the pace.

Rhyme: Most would not consider this a "rhyming poem" because it contains no end (external) rhymes. When read aloud, however, we discover the poem is rich with internal rhyme. Listen to the music of "the finger my grandfather lost to the auger" and "leaf-fall from the family tree."

Music: Alliteration, simply put, is the repetition of sounds. Assonance is the repetition of vowel sounds. Consonance is the repetition of consonant sounds. In reality, assonance and consonance are both a species of rhyme. Lyon's language is truly lyrical, meant to be heard: "spilling old pictures, / a sift of lost faces / to drift beneath my dreams."

Specific Detail/Proper Names: Lyon gets specific. She says "fudge" instead of "candy." She says "Clorox" instead of "bleach." She uses the proper names of things, which makes her images more specific and also adds to the poem's sound: *forsythia, Dutch elm, carbontetrachloride, Imogene* and *Alafair*.

Vivid Images: Vivid images call one or more of the reader's five senses into play. The reader *smells* the strong coffee, *feels* the cotton balls, *tastes* the dirt, *hears* the church verses, *sees* the forsythia and the photographs.

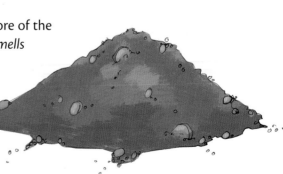

Line Breaks: The lines turn intentionally whether "end stopped" or "run on," and the words that hang along the poem's right margin are all very strong and visual.

Sense of Conclusion: Some poems can conclude with a sense of summation, when the poet ties together all the poem's details into a neat package: "I took the one less traveled by / and that has made all the difference" ("Road Not Taken" by Robert Frost). Other poems conclude in a more open-ended way, leaving the reader to wonder over a mystery, ponder a predicament, or consider new questions. "Tell me, what is it you plan to do / with your one wild and precious life?" ("The Summer Day" by Mary Oliver).

Now It's Your Turn

Write your own "Where I'm From" poem.

George Ella Lyon's poem "Where I'm From" shows how each of us is "from" more than just a place. We are from all the memories, experiences, and details that have shaped us into what we have become. The "where" of Lyon's poem is much more than a city or a town. Lyon's poem describes the past, but there's no reason that your poem can't refer to the present if you wish. It's your call.

To get the images flowing, first make a list of the following:

- Familiar sights, sounds, and smells of your home and neighborhood

- Familiar foods, from holidays, celebrations, or everyday meals

- Familiar sayings and expressions you've heard

- Family traditions that have shaped your home life

- Other details: relatives' names, religious experiences, common objects, street names, hiding places, plants growing in the yard, favorite books, songs, movies, or television shows

Reread Lyon's poem one more time. Listen to how she repeats and varies the phrase "I am from." See how she arranges her montage of images and keeps any judgmental comments to a minimum. Note her use of specific detail, proper names, and rich-sounding language.

Now grab your pen or laptop and write your own version.

The Poet's Decisions

So you've got all the necessary poetry tools, and you've got a good idea what to write about. This next section will address all the decisions that poets must make as they transform their ideas into poems. When writing a poem from scratch, the best way to begin is to write down the details. Grab your pen, and as you consider your topic, write down a simple list of hodgepodge details. Don't concern yourself, at first, with structure. You'll be surprised how a poem will come to life and crawl out from the depths of the descriptive rubble.

Details, Details

I can still remember (with horror) the first time I met Carrie Collier's parents. I was 13. Carrie was my first girlfriend, and I was invited to her house for dinner. In the first stanza of my poem, "Meeting Mom and Dad," I wanted to show how nervous I was.

I could have begun simply with straightforward commentary like this:

> **As I sat on the couch, at your parent's house**
> **I was extremely nervous.**

The words tell us a few things, but show us nothing. My job as a poet is to make the scene more vivid through detail:

> **Cool and thick the plastic sticks**
> **to the sweat on the back of my legs.**
> **I fidget on your parent's couch,**
> **with its waxy protection**
> **clinging to cushions and folds.**

"Hey," you might ask, "is this poem about meeting your girlfriend's parents, or meeting their sofa?" Well, it's both really. By describing the plastic-covered couch, I can imply a sneaky parallel to the mother and father's protective nature. Notice, too, how the more detailed version never uses the word "nervous," and yet, because of the details, (the sweating and fidgeting) the nervousness is undeniable.

Improve Your Eye for Details

Every poet is a poet in training. Even professional, published poets who have been writing poems for years are poets in training. By simply paying close attention, poets can train their minds to see details that the typical no-po person might miss.

A simple way to hone your descriptive ability is to practice seeing without your eyes and hearing without your ears. To do this, you'll need to close your eyes (or wear a blindfold) as you go about a few normal day-to-day tasks: getting dressed, signing your name, brushing your teeth, playing an instrument, riding in a car, walking outside, running, kicking a ball, making a sandwich, eating lunch. Without your sight your other senses will kick into overdrive, and you will begin to hear, smell, feel, and taste things better. Try listening to the radio more and watching television less. Or practice imagining your own scenes as you listen to the television without watching it.

Likewise, you can deprive your sense of sound by using earplugs as you move through your day. Try watching television for a while without the sound. Many visual details come to light with the sound turned down. You may be surprised at how well you can follow what's happening.

As you go about your day, don't simply look at things; observe them. Remind yourself that you are collecting details for later use. You are the reconnaissance probe, sent from another planet to explore this strange world called Earth. You have been equipped with five senses and a brain. Now if only you could remember where you put your pencil … Ah, details!

This Poem Has Been Brought to You By Your Five Senses

Warm pajamas, burps, kazoos,
stars, hot chocolate, I love yous,
perfume, popcorn, comfy shoes,
a hundred different blues.

Fresh-mown grass, hugs, puppy fur,
flowers, sunsets, kitten purrs,
after-bedtime whispered words,
wobbly newborn birds.

Observations & Explosions

Awareness. Intuition. An ear for language. An eye for detail. These combined powers of observation help the poet notice even the most miniscule of poetic moments. And this leads us to the poet's next big decision. Which of the many poetic "blooms" will make the best poem? Consider this: sometimes the most extraordinary poems spring from the most ordinary subjects. You might say it's the poet's job to transform seemingly insignificant "blooms" into—boom!—significant poems. Take a look at the following poem by William Carlos Williams.

The Red Wheelbarrow

so much depends
upon

a red wheel
barrow

glazed with rain
water

beside the white
chickens.

—William Carlos Williams

It seems at first that very little is happening in this poem. A poem about a *wheelbarrow*? How unglamorous can you get? Ah, but the poet, watching from his secret room, sees the scene for what it truly is. In the world of the barnyard, the wheelbarrow is an important resident. The wheelbarrow is dressed in royal red and adorned with a jeweled glaze of rainwater. On a farm, so much really does depend on rainwater. The poet looks upon this mundane barnyard event and sees healthy crops, abundant food, and a good life, and the chickens provide an endless supply of omelets.

Poets are, if nothing else, observant. But we're not observant like a private detective or a news reporter is observant. Detectives and reporters arrive to investigate a scene only after they are told something has happened. But poets are already on the scene *while* something is happening because scenes *follow* poets wherever they go—just like Mary's lamb. The simple fact is that something is *always* happening. The poet's first job is to see it.

Within the 10-foot circle around the chair I am sitting in, I can see hundreds of poems waiting to be written. There's a yogurt container now filled with pens and pencils. There's a half-full coffee mug, the Wright Brothers mug I bought in Kitty Hawk, North Carolina. There's a calendar turned to the wrong month. There's a book I'll never read. My chair has a broken spring and tilts me to the left. There's an already empty bag of Halloween candy my wife bought for the trick-or-treaters, though Halloween is still a week away! I have mice in my walls. My feet are cold. I can hear the sound of a skateboard outside. (It sounded like what skateboarders call an *ollie*. And it sounded like he missed.)

If the poet's first job is to see what's happening, the poet's second job is to "explode" it. Remember what Barry Lane said: the observant poet must "explode the moment" by transforming a seemingly insignificant object or event into something larger or more complex.

Project Your Image!

Here's a good poetry rule of thumb: the more sensory images your poem includes, the more imagination your readers use. Let's first look at a poem with minimal imagery and go from there. The poem "Rough," is a simple statement really, with little or no sensory details or images. We've seen this poem earlier in the book (on page 15) as an example of a unrhymed poem, but it's worth repeating here:

Rough

My life had gone
completely to the dogs
until the day I discovered
(to my astonishment)
that I was a dog myself.
Life was better after that.

This quirky poem is written in an easy style that mimics everyday speech. Nothing in the words causes the reader to imagine any specific sensory details (besides maybe picturing a dog or two).

Now let's consider a poem that relies heavily on sensory images. Look again at the first stanza of "Where I'm From" by George Ella Lyon on page 41.

To explain where she comes from, Lyon treats us to a mixture of images from her past. She doesn't simply tell us the name of a place; she shows us the sights, sounds, smells, and even the taste of the memories that were born there.

Your words can be powerful, but the images your words create are what move readers the most. One well-chosen descriptive image can say more than an entire page of explanation. Images are capable of succeeding where words sometimes fail. And because your readers have to use their own imaginations to conjure and consider the images for themselves, they become a very engaged audience.

Place Your Poems on the Accessibility Scale

We've all read poems that leave us scratching our heads. Take a look at an excerpt from "silence…" by E. E. Cummings:

silence

.is
a
looking

bird:the

turn
ing;edge,of
life

(inquiry before snow
—E. E. Cummings

A poem's degree of accessibility (how easy or difficult it is to understand) can be placed on a scale from 1 to 10. On the accessibility scale, I'd place "silence" at about 2. Let's look at a poem on the other end of the scale.

A Word is Dead

A word is dead
When it is said,
Some say.

I say it just
Begins to live
That day.
    —*Emily Dickinson*

I'd place Dickinson's "A Word is Dead" at about 8 on the accessibility scale.

As a poet, you must make the choice. How accessible do you want your poems to be? Less accessible poems may benefit from their added complexity; some readers (like me) enjoy reading poems that are a bit of a challenge. But remember, the less accessible your poem is, the harder your readers must work to make sense of it. Make them work too hard and your readers will just say "huh?" and move on to the next poem.

Point of View

It is popular these days to assume the "speaker" of a poem and the author of a poem are one and the same. But that is not always the case. Why not choose to write a poem from the point of view of someone or *something* else? Imagine a poem about air pollution from the point of view of the sky. Or a poem about bullies from a bully's point of view. It can be fun to take on the role of someone or *something* else and leave yourself behind. The result is called a *persona poem*, a poem in the voice and point of view of a speaker other than the poet.

That said, you have three basic points of view to choose from: first person (I walked alone); second person (you walked alone); and third person (the poet walked alone). First person is the most, uh, personal. Third person is the least personal.

Tense

As a rule, poems in present tense have a greater sense of immediacy and suspense than poems in the past tense. For example:

Past Tense

The woods were dark.
I walked alone.
I heard a noise.
I froze.

Present Tense

The woods are dark.
I walk alone.
I hear a noise.
I freeze.

The past tense example is the story of something that once happened. The present tense example gives readers the sense that the story is unfolding as they read. You can sometimes switch from one tense to another to change the intensity and pace of a poem. In the example below, I accentuate the switch with an appropriate line break.

Past into Present

The woods were dark.
I walked alone.

I hear a noise.
I freeze.

You can combine the intensity of present tense with the second person point of view to make your readers feel as if they are inside the poem itself.

Present Tense, Second Person

The woods are dark.
You walk alone.
You hear a noise.

You freeze.

Do you like how I separated "You freeze" from the rest of the poem? See how the last line now looks frozen and alone. Aren't I clever?

Form

Before Johannes Gutenberg invented a versatile printing press in the 1450s, poets had it easy. Back then, when a poet wanted to share his work, he (they were mostly men) would simply stand on a big rock and start reciting. To write out multiple copies of his poem by hand would have taken a roomful of monks, and besides, most of the people in his audience couldn't read.

So the poet spoke, and the audience listened. Everybody sensed the shape of the poem from the cadence of its delivery. Everyone knew where one line ended and another began because the line typically "turned" on a rhyme, like an Olympic swimmer doing kick-flips at the end of the pool, finishing one length and beginning another.

But the modern-day poet's job is more involved. In addition to its life as spoken sound, poetry has another life as it appears on the page. For our purposes, we can define the form of a poem simply as "the way the poem looks." As a poet, you can choose from two general categories of form: closed or open.

Closed Forms

Closed forms of poetry have rules that dictate a poem's shape, sound, meter, and sometimes even subject. The sonnet and the haiku are probably the most well known of the closed forms.

SONNET

A Cat Can Lounge Around All Day

A cat can lounge around all day, and lick
her fur, and yawn, and stretch, then circle round
and round about her nap-time spot to pick
the best position there is to be found.
And so she'll sleep and yawn a few hours more
and stretch and lick. Then at the door she'll frown
and wail as if to wake the dead before
she leaves to find a place to lie back down.
To say that cats are lazy isn't fair.
They sleep 'cause rest is something they require
to gain the strength for walking here and there.
When tired, it's in their nature to retire.
And that's why I avoid work conscience-free:
'Cause laziness comes natural to me.

HAIKU

Nothing in the cry
of cicadas suggests they
are about to die
—*Basho*

No matter who writes a sonnet, as long as the poet follows the rules, the end result will look like the example on the previous page. As you might have noticed, teachers are crazy about closed-form poetry. How many haikus, bio poems, and acrostics have you been asked to write over the years? Perhaps a few of you have even been asked to try your hand at the villanelle or sestina. There are even more closed forms. Some, like the double-dactyl and the clerihew, are so obscure even your teachers may not have heard of them.

Closed forms are especially handy for poets who are experiencing page fright—that panicky feeling you get by looking at a blank page or computer screen. When page fright hits, the paint-by-numbers ease of a closed-form poem can be a wonderful thing. It requires you to use your right brain—the creative side—to explore your subject while you use your left brain—the logical side—to follow the form's rules properly. It's the writer's equivalent of rubbing your tummy while patting your head. The resulting poem can be an end in itself, or a prewriting activity that could lead you to an entirely different poem.

Open Forms (Free Verse)

Writing closed-form poetry is kind of like being dressed up in a tux and tails. A little stiff, not so much room to move. Open-form, or free-verse, poetry, on the other hand, gives you a chance to let your hair down and dress to express your mood.

The term *free verse*, derived from the French *vers libre*, refers to poetry written without a specific (or even recognizable) meter. That's not to say the lines of a free-verse poem are haphazardly "stacked." It's just that the free-verse poet gets to determine meter and line breaks on a poem-by-poem basis, "free" from the rules and regulations of any set form. The twentieth century saw the dawn of free-verse poetry, and while closed forms of poetry are still showing up in modern publications, many established poets writing today have embraced free verse as their form of choice.

Shaping Words into a Poem

Very often, it's the shape or look of a poem that attracts readers' attention. Your poetry takes on whatever shape you want when you make choices about the length of the poem's lines. Wherever you stop a line is called a line break.

Here's what "The Red Wheelbarrow" (see page 47) looks like without any line breaks:

So much depends upon a red wheelbarrow, glazed with rainwater beside the white chickens.

The entire poem is really just one measly little sentence disguised as a poem. Without its form, Williams' poem looks kind of like a fancy cat that just came in out of the rain. You can see the poem for what it really is—simple naked words.

Now, you can begin to arrange these simple words—to shape them into a poem and, thus, fluff up the rain-soaked cat. When it comes to line breaks, the poet has two basic options: end-stopped lines and run-on lines.

End-Stopped Lines

End-stopped lines end in the same place where any speaker might naturally pause due to grammar or punctuation. Had Williams chosen to use end-stopped lines, his poem might look something like this:

> **So much depends**
> **upon a red wheelbarrow,**
> **glazed with rainwater**
> **beside the white chickens.**

Notice how Williams' original ho-hum sentence now has the appearance of intentional order, like soup cans arranged into a pleasing sales display. This would have been just fine, yet Williams knew that his poem's form could do more to illustrate the poem's subject. So he continued to try other things. Which brings us, now, to a poetic device that many free-verse poets regularly keep in their poet's toolbox: the run-on line.

Run-On Lines

If read aloud, end-stopped lines sound the way we speak. Run-on (also called *enjambed*) lines have a less tidy sound. They end where the poet feels it's most effective for them to end, rather than waiting for the natural pause of a period or comma. Because run-on lines don't break where the reader might naturally pause, the pull is greater from line to line and provides a sense of anticipation and movement. We can reshape Williams' words into run-on lines like this:

> **So much depends**
> **upon a red wheel**
> **barrow, glazed with rain**
> **water beside the white**
> **chickens.**

Read the lines out loud, pausing slightly at the end of each line, and you'll begin to hear the sound of a wheelbarrow's single wheel as it lurches across the farmyard.

End-Stopped vs. Run-On: You Decide!

Take one of your poems and rewrite it with end-stopped line breaks, and then write it again with run-on line breaks. Read each version out loud. Exaggerate the pauses and listen for differences in rhythm and flow. You may find that the end-stopped lines give a sense of closure, while the run-on lines give a sense of suspense, effectively pulling the reader from one line to the next. Which works best for the poem?

Final Thoughts on "The Red Wheelbarrow"

Notice how Williams altered the poem's shape to create an additional visual dimension. He divides his lines into four two-line stanzas, with three words in the first line and one word on the second. This increases the poem's look of intentional order and transforms the stacked lines into a pleasing visual effect of four tiny wheelbarrows, with the first line acting as the handle and the second as the "bowl." And because of the words' somewhat loping rhythm, caused by the run-on lines, the poem even sounds like its subject.

The Red Wheelbarrow

so much depends
upon

a red wheel
barrow

glazed with rain
water

beside the white
chickens.

Play with Structure

Poetry can be as much a visual art as it is a written art. What your poem looks like on the page can determine how the words are read. Readers don't just read a poem for content; they also follow visual cues suggested by the poem's printed form.

Don't be afraid to let your words play on the page. Let them line up like soldiers on parade. Let them dash down stairs. Let them fall fast and crash on the grass. Or skip from rock to rock across a stream. To emphasize a word, make it live alone on its very own line. Add stanza breaks to make the reader stop. Play with punctuation. Ellipses make the words trail off. Parentheses add subtlety to a sly aside. Indent a line to expand on the thought of the line that came before. Let your words build and explode. Let them linger in the air. Let them slink away slowly till they're barely even there.

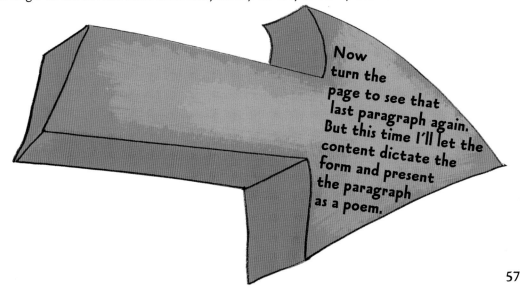

Now turn the page to see that last paragraph again. But this time I'll let the content dictate the form and present the paragraph as a poem.

Don't Be Afraid

to   let   your   words
play   on   the   page.
Let   them   line   up
like   soldiers on   parade.

Let
    them
        dash
           down
               stairs.
                    Let
                    them
                    fall
                    fast
                    and
                    CRASH on the grassssss.
Or skip   from rock to   rock across   a   stream.

To emphasize a word, make it live
alone
on its very own line.
Add stanza breaks or dashes to make the reader stop—

Play with punctuation.
Ellipses make the words trail off...
Parentheses add subtlety (to a sly aside).
Indent a line
          to expand on the thought
               of the line that came before.

Let your words build and explode!

    them   in   air.
Let   linger   the

Let them slink away
s l o w l y
till they're barely even there.

Try this yourself. Grab a paragraph from a favorite book or even this book and play with its structure. Read the resulting "poem" out loud, paying attention to the pauses and line breaks.

A Demonstration

Now comes the moment of truth—where all the decisions come together. By now you have everything you need to create a poem. It's time to start writing.

And just to prove that I would never ask someone to write what I would not write myself, I'll go first! Working without a safety net, I (a real poet) will now create a real poem before your very eyes. And you, eager reader, get to watch over my shoulder every step of the way.

I have no idea what my topic will be. I have no idea whether it will rhyme or not. I have no idea whether it will be long or short, funny or serious, easy or difficult. And I certainly don't know whether it will be brilliant, stinky, or indifferent. Who cares? Writin' poems feels good.

All these decisions to make! How do you keep them all in your head when you're writing a poem? Well, for one thing, you don't. The more you read and write, the more these decisions become second nature to you as a poet. Just do what feels right, and don't be afraid to tinker with what you've written.

Watch Me Go Boom

Look around. What poems do you see? Are you in your bedroom? Is your bed made? If it's made, who made it? If it's not, why not? And what do the sheets look like? Are they mountains? And if so, are they the Rockies or the Appalachians? Are they waves? And if so, are they ripples or tsunamis? Now jump in. Are you sailing? Are you surfing? What if you're drowning? And if you're drowning, why? A person doesn't drown in a bed! How is the bed connected to your life? The bed is more than a bed, but what?

Now that I've got a good stream of questions to juggle, I'll grab a pen and paper and start writing. I'll begin with simple concrete descriptions and "explode" from there. Hold on tight, we're about to write our way to a poem!

> **The covers are blue and the white**
> **of the sheets is like white-capped waves**
> **that drag me under. Hold me in.**
> **Won't let me go**
> **and drown me in sweet sleep.**

Somehow, as I describe the tangled bedsheets, I come up with the metaphor of the sea as bed. Now, let's start asking some "what if" questions. For example, what if I just walk ashore?

> **To walk ashore would be**
> **to go to school and face another day.**

Wait a minute. I don't dread all days. Let me revisit that last line. I decide to choose my worst day, Monday, and make it "land-locked" Monday to continue my ocean theme.

> **To walk ashore would be**
> **to go to school and face**
> **another land-locked Monday**

Another "what if" comes to mind. What if I don't walk ashore? What if I stay right where I am in the safety of the sheets? And so I add a tidy ending to my impromptu poem.

> **Instead I'll dive beneath**
> **the waves and sleep.**

But on second thought, this ending seems a little too cute. It resolves the poem, in its tidy way, but I don't think that's what I want. I think I want to leave it a little fuzzy. Leave the reader with a sense of mystery—will the narrator choose the bed/waves or the Monday/shore? So I remove the last two lines almost as quickly as I add them. I also cut out a few unnecessary words in the first stanza.

> **The covers, blue and white-capped waves**
> **drag me under. Hold me in.**
> **Won't let me go**
> **and drown me in sweet sleep.**
>
> **To walk ashore would be**
> **to go to school and face**
> **another land-locked Monday**

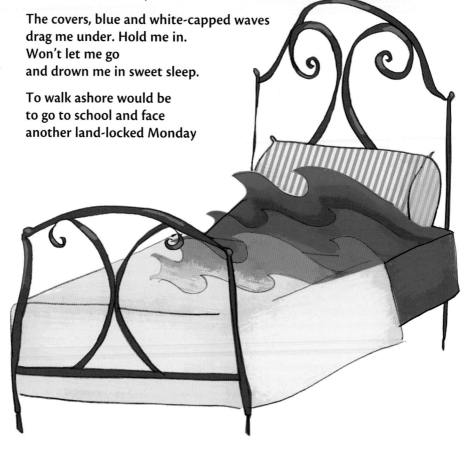

Now it's time to play with rhythm. I rewrite the first four lines to make them read like the rhythm of the waves. The punctuation and capital letters seem to stop the flow, so I remove both. I also rearrange the lines to give more emphasis to words beginning or ending with the "s" sound. For the same reason, I change "hold me in" to "hold me fast." The hissing sound of the "s," called sibilance, allows readers to hear the waves upon the sand. Also, in the final two lines, the term "land-locked Monday" makes the reference to school unnecessary, so I remove it.

> **the covers**
> **blue and white-capped waves**
> **drag me under hold me fast**
> **drown me in sweet sleep**
>
> **to walk ashore would be to face**
> **another land-locked Monday**

Two finishing touches: I decide to leave Monday capitalized in the "proper" way and add a period at the end of the poem to emphasize the feeling of being stopped, land-locked.

> **to walk ashore would be to face**
> **another land-locked Monday.**

Time to choose a title. Hmmm. "Bed" would do. I like the simplicity of "Bed." I might title it "Merman" to good sarcastic effect. Or I could title it "Poseidon," after the Greek god of the sea. I go with this third choice. At the last minute I decide to set the final line off by itself. I think it might help illustrate the separation of water and land. Why not? Now, let's take a good look at the final result.

> ## Poseidon
>
> **the covers**
> **blue and white-capped waves**
> **drag me under hold me fast**
> **drown me in sweet sleep**
> **to walk ashore would be to face**
>
> **another land-locked Monday.**

I notice that my poem includes two hyphenated phrases. "White-capped waves" is the opposite of "land-locked Monday." I didn't consciously create this parallel structure, but I love how it works, so I keep it. Now that I'm able to try reading the poem out loud, I notice that the title and all but the final line contain the "s" sound of the sea. Nice touch. I did it by accident, but I'll take credit for it anyway. The heavy, plodding sounds of the final line contrast the liquid hissing sound of the sea, just as Monday is, to me, the most plodding day of the week.

So There You Have It ...

An example of how a poet sees a scene (the bloom) and explodes the moment (the boom) to create a poem. As I wrote "Poseidon," I didn't really know where I was going until I got there. By questioning and "what-iffing" I found my own unique take on the scene. I could have stopped there. I had the metaphor. I had a poem. But to make it really sing, I kept going. I had to pull out more tools and make lots of decisions along the way. I didn't consult any poetry textbooks; I followed my gut.

The trick is to be fearless. Chisel and chop and blend until every word, every line, and every stanza is working as hard as it can. Don't let your words be slackers. The payoff? It's those happy accidents. Discovering that your brain knows more than you know. Connections that appear in your poems without you ever realizing you put them there. And, of course, it's knowing you just crafted a brilliant gem of a poem.

Now, it's your turn. Pen? Check. Paper? Check. Brain? Check. Ears? Check. Eyeballs? Check! Poet toolbox? Check. Now, stop thinking and start following your intuition. Look around you. Choose a bloom. Then start writing and make it go boom.

Revising Your Poems

I can almost hear your groan at the very mention of this despicable "revising" word. Teachers say it a lot, and they seem to say it just when you're feeling so proud of your perfectly perfect, finished final-draft, stick-a-fork-in-it-'cause-it's-done poem.

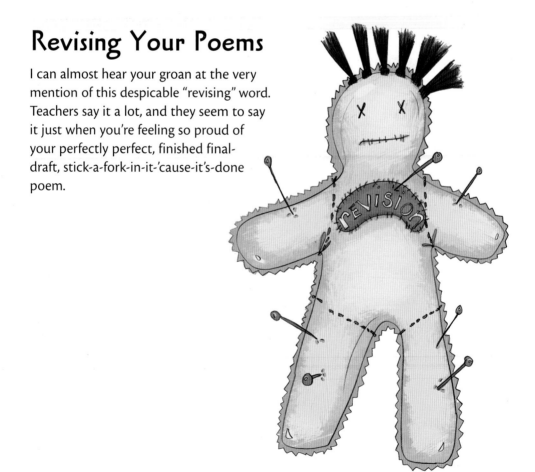

Reasons Many Poets Hate Revision

Been there; done that! It's like writing the same poem twice.

It takes twice the time to make my poem half as long.

If I revise my poem, the world as I know it will cease to exist.

My poems are perfect the way they are.

I don't like to waste paper.

Add your own reasons to your journal—I'm sure you have a bunch. It's healthy to be pleased with a poem you've written, but don't allow your ego to block your poems from reaching their full potential.

My Very Simple Revision Plan

Photocopy this short list and refer to it anytime you start getting discouraged about revising your poems. Why will this help? Because there are really only two ways to hone your revision skills:

1. Read a lot.

The more you read, the deeper your pool of experience will be, and the sharper your intuition will become.

2. Write a lot.

The more you write, the easier it becomes to rewrite. A poet who has written only one poem will spoil that poem like an only child. The more poems a poet has to care for, the less spoiled the poems will be.

Pretty simple, eh!?

Your Best Revising Tools

1. Time

It's very difficult to read a poem objectively on the day you wrote it. It's best to let it age—a day, a week, a month. After a good night's sleep, your perfect poem may not seem quite so perfect, as if ill-tempered poetry elves vandalized it while you slept.

2. An Audition

With poetry, there's no room for words that aren't pulling their weight. Make those words work for you. Make them prove they belong where they are. Force your words to audition for the page, and let them know that there are a hundred other words out there ready to take their spot the moment they show any sign of weakness.

3. A Sense of Fearless Tinkering

Don't be afraid to take apart what you've done. Be like the kid who takes his dad's stereo apart to see how it works. Take your poem apart and put it back together. Don't worry about the extra parts still on the floor. Make your last line your first line. Read your poem backwards. Cut out your favorite line. Cut and paste. Sure, save your previous version somewhere, so if you horribly mangle something you once loved, it's still available, but otherwise, cast your fears aside, take out your toolbox, and tinker away.

4. Highlighting the Poem's Golden Moments

Use a yellow highlighter to designate your poem's top three golden moments (be they a single word, a partial phrase, or an entire line) that are vital to the poem's life. A poem's golden moments are its essential organs (brain, heart, liver, and lungs) without which the poem could not survive.

Once you've highlighted the poem's golden moments, examine the remaining words with a critical eye. Can the less vital parts of the poem somehow be revitalized? Can they be replaced? Removed altogether? Try composing an entirely new poem that includes the three golden moments you salvaged from your original.

5. Vivacious Vocal Cords

Poetry is ultimately a spoken art. Written words are only shadows of spoken sound. Not only is reading aloud an appropriate way to share your work, but it's also a great revision tool. It helps flag a poem's awkward phrases, blips, bleeps, and blemishes. So stand up, poet-proud, and say your poems out loud.

Always Something to Write About

You don't need to use every tool in your toolbox to write cool poems. The poet's job is to decide which tools are right for the job. But don't let all this decision making freak you out. When pen meets paper (or fingers meet keys), you just need to go with the flow and follow your intuition.

In this next section, we will discuss the first major decision that every poet must face: what to write about. Luckily for us poets, would-be poems are always lurking near, usually right under our noses.

Celebrate the Mundane

from Delight

Something is going to happen, I tell you I know.
This morning, I tell you, I saw ice in the bucket.
Something is going to happen and you can't duck it.
The way the wind blows is the way the dead leaves go.
Something is going to happen, and I'm telling you so.

—*Robert Penn Warren*

Remember, as a poet, your first job is to gaze out the window of your secret room and watch for whatever "blooms" might catch your eye and inspire a poem. The blooms are everywhere (conversations, events, people, objects), but they may be things that non-poets take for granted. In "Delight," Robert Penn Warren sees a bloom in a bucket of ice, a bloom in the way dead leaves float on the wind. Some of the most significant poems are written about seemingly insignificant things—what non-poets might call mundane.

To Make a Prairie

To make a prairie it takes a clover and one bee,
One clover, and a bee,
And revery.
The revery alone will do
If bees are few.

—*Emily Dickinson*

Hamburger Haiku

Fast food Happy Meal.
Everybody is happy.
Except for the cow.

Write About a Radish...

Write about a radish
Too many people write about the moon.

The night is black
The stars are small and high
The clock unwinds its ever-ticking tune
Hills gleam dimly
Distant nighthawks cry.
A radish rises in the waiting sky.
—*Karla Kuskin*

In the non-poet (or *no-po*) world, the word *mundane* has unfortunately become synonymous with *boring*. But the word mundane actually originates from the Latin *mundos*, meaning "the world." So, in truth, mundane poems are poems about the world. And the world is anything but boring!

Truth is, sometimes poets are best able to explore lofty ideas through lowly subjects. Don't write about *love*. Write about holding hands. Don't write about *hate*. Write about the bullies who walk the halls at school. Even the simplest of poems can offer its reader a different way of seeing the world.

Journals: Your Storage Vault

I get a lot of good ideas in the shower. Something about the hot water relaxes my body and mind, and before I know it, I've got an idea. If I'm lucky, I'll remember it long enough to get it down on paper. Sometimes I do, sometimes I don't. But there are just as many times when I have nothing to write about and no matter how many showers I take, I've got nothing. Zip. Nada. That's when I turn to my vault—otherwise known as my journal (see page 32). Most writers I know have a journal (or several), and each person's journal is as individual as the person who keeps it. For instance, my journal has some dried-out leaves in it. It also contains doodles, newspaper clippings, great words I've discovered, and lists of funny things my kids say. Not everything I put in my journal will end up in a poem. But if something is interesting to me, I put it in. Who knows? I could have a germ of inspiration waiting in those pages. And when I'm stumped for an idea, it's a great place to visit.

There are no rules for keeping a journal, but I've come up with a checklist of things to consider. These work for me, but change them to suit your needs. All you're trying to do is create a place where you feel safe to express ideas and collect things you may be able to use down the road.

Awesome Journal Checklist

- Think of your journal as a vault where you can keep all those great/weird/horrible yet compelling/(insert your adjective here) ideas you have but don't have time to write about right away. When you do that, you can end up writing whatever you want. It can be a place to write letters you never send, a self-analysis, a sketchbook, a doodle notebook, a scrapbook … Basically, it's a place to express yourself and the world that you notice.

- The only way to do all this stuff comfortably is to keep the journal to yourself. I suggest not sharing it with anyone (even a best friend), otherwise you end up writing for somebody else. You needn't keep your journal in secret, but neither should you ever feel obligated to share its contents. If friends or family complain when you won't let them read your journal, just tell them they'll have to write their own.

- Don't feel like you have to write in it every day (even if you signed the pledge on page 26). The journal is for when you need it. If you start feeling guilty for not writing in it, then it's no longer any fun and it starts getting annoying.

- Don't criticize what's in your journal. Remember, it's only for you. No one else needs to know what's in there. And while you're at it, don't worry about crossing stuff out, writing neatly, or even spelling correctly. Who cares? Your journal is an official "no-spell zone." Garbled grammar welcome!

- Date your entries. It's fun to go back to old journals and read about who you used to be. Dated entries help give you a good sense of your own growth.

- Make lists freely. Writing lists is a quick way of organizing your thoughts and focusing on a single topic. Lists are brief and concise, so they're good practice for clear, confident writing. Making lists is also an excellent cure for poets who suffer from "sentence-fragment phobia." When it comes to writing lists, complete sentences need not apply.

Mind Games

Sometimes, just writing a poem (even from a prompt) seems too big a deal. Your brain screams, "You're trying to write a poem, for gosh sakes! This is important! Don't mess it up!" If this is happening, you'll never write a poem that you're happy with. What follows is a bunch of poetry activities to make your brain shut up. These are fun ways to get the ideas flowing and methods for tricking your brain into writing poetry.

MAGNETIC WORDS

This is a really interesting activity where you don't have to come up with any of your own words, and yet, when you're done, you've got yourself an original poem.

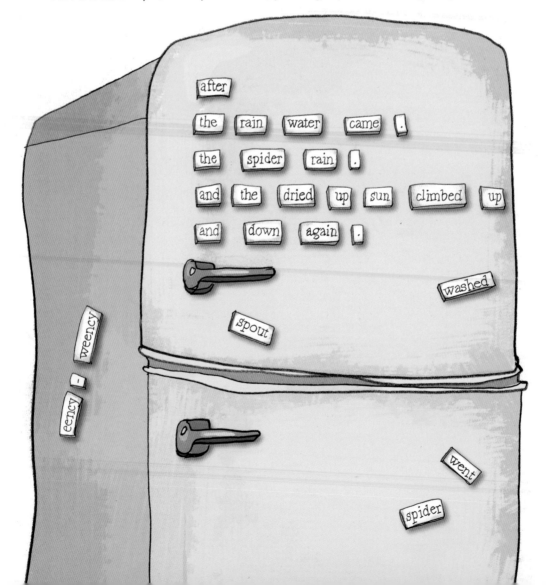

WHAT YOU NEED

- Computer and printer
- Printer-compatible magnetic paper
- Scissors
- Something metal

WHAT YOU DO

1. Look for poems, nursery rhymes, or songs that you like (or, even better, hate).

2. Type the words you've chosen in a fun font. Insert two spaces between each word you type and leave one and a half spaces between lines so it'll be easier to cut the words from the magnetic paper later on. Also type a bunch of punctuation marks. Adjust the document margins so that they measure 1/2 inch (1.3 cm) on all sides of the page, so you can make the most of each sheet of magnetic paper.

3. Print the page of words and punctuation marks onto a plain piece of printer paper and check for spaces, cut-off words, and any other problems you should fix before you print on the magnetic paper.

4. Set a sheet of magnetic paper in the printer tray, positioned so the white side of the paper will be printed on. If you're not sure whether the white side should face up or down in the tray, do a test run with a piece of scrap paper. Make an X on the paper, put the paper in the tray so the X is facing up, and print the page of words to see which side comes out blank and which gets printed on.

5. Cut the words from the magnetic paper. Save leftover scraps of the magnetic paper for words you might need as you create your poem.

6. Stick the words to something metallic (your locker, the refrigerator) and rearrange them to make new poems. Add new words (from more songs or nursery rhymes) from time to time for fresh vocabulary.

BEFORE

> The eency-weency spider climbed up the waterspout.
> Down came the rain and washed the spider out.
> Out came the sun and dried up all the rain.
> And, the eency-weency spider went up the spout again.

AFTER

> The rain water came.
> The spider rain.
> And the dried-up sun climbed up
> And down again.

Found Poems

Instead of coming up with words on your own, create a found poem by gathering words from your environment (trash, newspaper, magazines, signs, license plates, etc.) and assembling them into a poem. The world is full of snippets of language that go unnoticed. It's your job to rescue them from obscurity and put them center stage in a found poem.

You might discover that sometimes it's what *isn't* there that makes a found poem powerful. In September 1989 in Fitzgerald, Georgia, I found a note on the sidewalk in front of a middle school. The left and right sides of the note were missing. All that was left was the heart. I simply gave what I found a title.

Center Torn Out
—Remember yesterday—
—hard-headed woman—
—What did I do?—
—you up, but—
—walked away. I—
—you with my highest—
—as different if—
—kiss or something—
—don't even think—
—I really love you.—
—treat me this way.—
—I'll tell everything—
—I can prove it.—
—when I let you—
—You went and—
—about how I felt about—
—get in fights—
—you. And you just—
—necklace away—
—show every—
—if you—
—tell me—

NEWSPAPER POEM

Here's one really fun way to create found poetry. Make sure everyone's done reading the newspaper before tearing it up.

WHAT YOU NEED

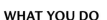

- Newspaper
- Scissors
- Tape or glue
- Paper

WHAT YOU DO

1. Grab yesterday's newspaper. Cut out at least 50 words and phrases that catch your attention. Don't cut out entire headlines or sentences (unless you find a real doozy). Hold on to the newspaper in case you need some punctuation or an extra word or two.

2. Lay out the pieces on a table and start arranging them. Create new words by taping together parts of real words, if you want.

3. Keep playing. Read your emerging poem out loud and listen to the words. Feel free not to make too much sense. Be open to the nonsense of your newspaper poem.

4. When you're completely satisfied with your poem, tape or glue the words to your paper. Pay attention to line breaks and any poetic devices that crop up.

Inspiration in the Strangest Places

Poems can come from just about anywhere. Here's a list of places where some of my poet friends and I have gotten ideas and inspiration:

- Fortune cookies
- Grocery lists
- Store receipts
- Ticket stubs
- Candy wrappers
- Advertisements
- Slogans
- Movie trailers
- Old e-mails
- Garbage found on the street

- Small valentine candy hearts
- E-mail spam
- Road signs

- Bumper stickers
- T-shirts
- Graffiti
- Newspaper headlines

- Magazine articles
- Gossip
- Photograph captions
- Notes passed during class (grab them from the trash when no one's looking)

Take a Hike

Go ahead and do what the title here says. But bring along your notebook, and write down a bunch of images, sounds, tastes, textures, and more from your observations. Keep each entry short—a single phrase will usually do—and don't worry about the "deeper meaning" of your observations. Your job is to act as the camera, recording snapshots of your day. Don't worry if the images seem jumbled. Poetry has a way of making sense of images that at first seem illogical together. Sometimes the connections in poetry only come when we turn our logical brains off. When you get home, play with your snapshots and see what you come up with.

Go on a Word/Image Outing

Take poetry field trips to visit interesting places and see unusual events. The best outings are the ones that combine vivid visuals plus written and spoken language. Suggestions: the zoo, the circus, a monster truck rally, an art/history/science museum, a skateboard park.

Letter Poem

Write a poem in the form of a letter addressing a person, place, thing, or even a character in a book.

Malcolm, My Man

Malcolm (my man!)
You don't know me.
But I know you.
I dream of you.
In your blackness I see myself.
I long to be the man you once were.
What you are.
Who you are.
That is all that matters to you.
You're like no one I've ever known.
I see all in your eyes.
Malcolm (my man!)
Man with no fear,
No boundaries.
Show me the way.
Damn!
Malcolm, you had so far to go.
Death, so bloody.
Still it was a gift.
The end was inevitable and so was your memory.
True men live forever.
That is the way it will always be. Forever.
Never forgotten.
That is what I want to be.

—*Duane Shorter*

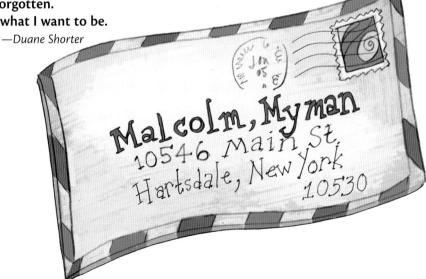

Malcolm, My man
10546 Main St.
Hartsdale, New York
10530

A Natural Self-Portrait

Create a list of your characteristics, including who you are, what you're like, and even what you look like. Next, choose an object in nature that you feel shares common characteristics with you. Make a list of other characteristics of the natural object. Now try writing a poem that illustrates the comparison. If you want, you can start by simply saying, "I am like ... "

Tree of Life

Soil of birth and life,
Feedings, nurturing of roots,
Supplying strength needed to grow,
Climbing, working, upward the trunk,
Gaining knowledge,
Branches reaching, grasping at goals,
Spreading my leaves to the sky.

—Daniel Greene

As the Green Grass Grows

So have I
Nurtured by my parents to keep me on a level playing field
If left unattended running wild and free
Drinking in the softness of a spring shower
Fearing the brutality of a summer drought or hurricane
Sheltering friends and loved ones as the lush green lawn offers refuge
To Mother Nature's tiny creatures
Whispering my dreams as the blades of grass sway gently in the autumn breeze
Concealing innermost thoughts in the quiet shady corners of my life
Celebrating successes in the sun-drenched pastures of learning
Drowning my sorrows in the weeds outside my bedroom window
Always seeking to grow
Believing I'll always have a yard or two to gain

—Peg Marlette

Inquisition

Write down a list of questions to ask someone (or something) you encounter. You can speak directly to the subject or ask the questions generally. This list of questions might prove to be a poem in itself, or it may trigger a poem that provides an answer to one or more of the questions.

White Goat

White Goat, is your name Billie?
What are you thinking as you
Twist your head around the feeding bin?
Do you miss your kids?
Are they crying for you?
Will you be with them ever again?

—*Cheryl Bromley Jones*

Mystery Poem

Write a "Who Am I?" or a "What Am I?" poem in which the speaker only gives descriptive clues, and the reader must guess who, or what, the speaker is. The answer can be given as part of the poem's ending or not at all. The poem can take whatever form you choose.

The Mountain Chicken

I'm called the Mountain Chicken
even though I never cluck.
You'll find me in Dominica
if you have any luck.
I do not peck. I do not scratch.
My name must be a joke.
I do not strut. Instead I hop.
I do not cluck. I croak.
Don't look inside the chicken coop.
I'm underneath this log.
I'm really not a chicken, see
I really am a...

Who Am I?

I played a sport, Round Ball the game.
I flew through the air, and all knew my name.
To the greatest heights, I did reach,
When playing with the dream, this—no one could teach.
The size of the ball did change but once,
And to the larger did I return.
From fame and glory did I retire,
Wearing red and black attire.
Who am I?

—P.J. Purdy and Tammy Roberts

Riddle

We are little airy creatures,
All of different voice and features:
One of us in glass is set,
One of us is found in jet,
One of us is set in tin,
One a lump of gold within;
If the last you should pursue,
It can never fly from you.

—Author unknown

Metaphors

I'm a riddle in nine syllables,
An elephant, a ponderous house,
A melon strolling on two tendrils,
O red fruit, ivory, fine timbers!
This loaf's big with its yeasty rising.
Money's new-minted in this fat purse.
I'm a means, a stage, a cow in calf.
I've eaten a bag of green apples,
Boarded the train there's no getting off.

—Sylvia Plath

Answers: The Mountain Chicken: frog; Who Am I?: Michael Jordan;
Riddle: vowels; Metaphors: pregnant

Concrete Poem

Write a "shape poem" in which the words of the poem visually represent the subject of the poem. A poem about leaves might be in the shape of a leaf, for example.

Poetree

A treetop
is a magic thing,
a home for wind and fur and wings.
A place where squirrels can make a nest.
A stop where weary birds can rest.
A home for wind and fur and wings,
a treetop is a magic thing.

Tree trunks
stand up straight
and long. They're
rough. They're
tough and very
strong. They
branch out spring
and summertime
so kids can have
a place to climb.

The hide-away half of the tree
is the half of the tree you can't see.
The hide-away half underground
grows its root without making a sound.
The hide-away half down below
spreads as wide as the top as it grows.
The hide-away half of the tree can be found
living all of its hide-away life upside down.

Write a Limerick

A limerick is a five-line poem, usually funny, arranged in an A-A-B-B-A rhyme pattern. Lines one and two consist of eight or nine syllables. Lines three and four consist of five or six syllables. The last line (which rhymes with the first two) consists of from eight to 10 syllables. Limericks can be used to tell brief stories or to describe the characteristics of something.

Variety

A chameleon when he's feeling blue,
Can alter his glum point of view.
By changing his hue
To a color that's new:
I'd like to do that, wouldn't you?
—*Eve Merriam*

Said an envious, erudite ermine:
"There's *one* thing I cannot determine:
When a *man* wears my coat,
He's a person of note.
While *I'm* but a species of vermin!"
—*Oliver Herford*

Faster Than Light

There was a young lady named Bright,
Whose speed was much faster than light.
She went out one day
In a relative way
And returned on the previous night.
—*A.H. Reginald Buller*

Try writing your own limericks. Instead of writing an essay on your summer vacation, how about turning it into a limerick! What else can you write a limerick about? An experience with a friend? Something funny your pet does? Your least favorite class? Why you didn't do your homework? An embarrassing (yet amusing) moment?

Write a Cinquain

A cinquain is a five-line unrhymed poem that usually follows this pattern:

Line one: One noun that introduces the poem's subject. This line can be the title.

Line two: Two adjectives that describe the subject.

Line three: Three verbs that relate to the subject.

Line four: Four-word phrase that tells the writer's feelings or describes the subject.

Line five: One noun (different from line one) that sums up the previous four lines.

Give one a try the next time you have an idea but don't know what to write about it.

Grackles

Iridescent, black
Splashing, hopping, dunking
Fluttering feathered creek communion
Bath time

Heron

White, long-necked
Watching, wading, eating
Segregated from the others
Fisherman
—Joy Ray

Multi-Voice Poem

Write a two-voice poem—perhaps a conversation between two (or more) speakers. Your two voices can speak at the same time or alternate, passing the lines back and forth.

Snail

Snail upon the wall,
Have you got at all
Anything to tell
About your shell?
Only this, my child—
When the wind is wild,
Or when the sun is hot,
It's all I've got.
—John Drinkwater

Write a Prose Poem

Is it prose or is it poetry? Prose writing has come to include every type of writing that is NOT poetry: essays, novels, short stories, reports, nonfiction, and so on. But writers of prose use many of the same tools that poets use (metaphor, repetition, alliteration, rhythm, sometimes even rhyme). In fact, some writing exists in a gray area that melds poetry and prose so thoroughly that it becomes a genre of its own—prose poetry.

Generally speaking, prose poetry refers to poems that have no specified line breaks—the poem's words are confined only by the page's margins. Typically, prose poems are not longer than a page. Because they lack the usual line breaks, prose poems can sound rambling and chatty. But when it is well written, a prose poem can take a reader on a nonstop ride, captured by the poem's rolling rhythm and intensity.

Cousin Zane Runs Screaming in Terror Through the House, A Victim of Our Practical Joke

Only the *children* living in a house know its many tricks: how to climb the counter for cookies; which of the stairs has a tendency to squeak. My brother and I discovered early on the secret of the family bathroom; that slamming the bathroom door with a bang would cause the medicine cabinet to open on its own. A demonstration in sound waves, air, and latent energy I guess.

I agree. It was a nasty gag to play on one's own cousin. But looking back, our story was so improbable. Who in their right mind, would have believed us? That the medicine chest was haunted by a ghost, not just evil, but allergic to sound? And every time you'd slam the door, the spirit would sneeze the cabinet open—creaking on its hinges? Who would have believed?

So that was the basic set up. Our cousin's visit was terror and tears. From his fear we learned the potential power of our stories and how reality is merely a servant to words. It is in this scene that I realized my calling as a poet: The Bathroom cabinet come to life. My cousin Zane, his thin white arms outstretched, in mortal flight from some fancy of my imagination.

Collaborative Poems

There are lots of ways to write poems with friends, family, and even teachers.

The E-mail Poem

To start the poem, write down one word and send it to a friend. That friend writes down the next word to the poem, and sends it back to you. You add the next two words and send it back, and so on until you both think the poem is done. Once you get to seven or eight words each, start working backward until you're back to writing one word each. Of course, you can do this with a piece of paper instead of e-mail.

The Exquisite Corpse Poem

This is a great name for a cool poetry activity. The surrealists (a twentieth-century group of artists who attempted to express the working of the subconscious mind) played this game, and often published their exquisite corpses. (In case you are just dying to know, the name comes from a famous line from an early example of this entertaining form: "The exquisite corpse will drink the young wine." Creepy, eh?)

THE ONE-PAGE VERSION

Gather your friends together (the more the merrier). Write two opening lines of a poem at the top of a sheet of paper. Fold the sheet back so only the second line shows. Pass it to the next poet, who, only being able to read your second line, adds her own two lines to the poem. She folds the paper again so only her second line shows, and this continues until everyone has had a turn. You can keep passing the paper around until it is filled. Then, of course, someone has to read it! After reading your one-of-a-kind exquisite corpse, write the poem's "birthdate" at the bottom of the page followed by the signatures of all the contributors. This is a great way to capture a fun moment from the past. And, as always, you just might find a poem of your own lurking within the lines of the exquisite corpse.

THE PAGE-PER-POET VERSION

Follow the same rules as above, but this time everyone gets a piece of paper. Each poet writes the first two lines of a poem and folds the sheet back so only the second line shows. Each poem in progress is then put in the center of the group, and poets take turns picking up poems, adding lines, and folding. When everyone's done, have a poetry reading. Be as dramatic as possible.

The He Said/She Said Poem

If you have ever found yourself scratching your head in confusion during a futile attempt to understand the opposite sex, this is the poem for you. The title of this enlightening two-stanza poem indicates the chosen topic: love, clothes, cars, friendship, sports, herbal tea, nose hair, etc. The subtitle of the first stanza is "He said." The subtitle of the second stanza is "She said." Or vice versa. All you need for this poem is one poet of each gender (or not), or poets can divide themselves into male and female "teams." Simply agree upon a prompt that will open both poems (i.e., "Fun is … " "The trouble with friendship is … " "I like being a girl/boy because … "). Also agree upon a basic form, such as five lines. Write your poems at the same time and then compare the results.

Here's an example I wrote with poet Sara Holbrook:

Fun

He Said
Fun is a joyride,
a spitting competition,
telling bad jokes,
laughing till our sides ache,
knowing that we all belong.

She Said
Fun is a giggle,
pink lipstick, blue nail polish,
whispering girlfriends,
a good cry at a movie,
then laughing
  all the way home.

Tribute Poem

A tribute poem is a poem that uplifts one of your heroes. Think about why this person is worthy of praise—not just the big reasons, but the little reasons, too. Your hero may have a special skill. Perhaps your hero did some amazing deed in the past. Or perhaps your hero does something special every day. Can you think of an appropriate metaphor you could use to describe your hero?

Don't write about someone famous (an athlete, a president, an actor, a writer); write about a hero you know personally. A tribute poem about someone who is close to you rings truer than one about some famous person you've never met.

from Mama's Magic

My Mama is protection
like those quilts her mother used to make.
She tucked us in with cut out history all around us.
We found we could walk anywhere
in this world and not feel alone.
My Mama never whispered the shame of poverty in our ears.
She taught us to dance to our own shadows.
"Pay no attention to those grand parties
on the other side of the tracks."

"Make your own music," she'd say
as she walked,
as she cleaned
the sagging floorboards of that place.
"You'll get there."
"You'll get there."
Her broom seemed to say with every wisp.
We were my Mama's favorite recipe.
She whipped us up in a big brown bowl
supported by her big brown arms.
We were homemade children.
Stitched together with homemade love.

—Glenis Redmond

Jump Starts

Looking for something to get your writing jump-started? Need something new and different to write about? Poetry prompts could be just the thing for you. A prompt is just something to get you started. Once you're off and running, you can totally ignore what the prompt was asking you to do in the first place. It's up to you.

How to Work with These Prompts

1. Grab your journal and a pen. For me, prompts don't work as well when I do them on a computer, but give it a try if you want.

2. Look at the prompts on the next several pages. Choose one that gets your attention.

3. Give yourself at least 15 minutes. Use a timer if you have one. Start writing. Don't pick your pen up off the page. Just write and write and write. If you have to write, "I have nothing to write about!" a bunch of times, then do it. Don't stop until your time is up.

Some Cool Prompts

Not every one of these prompts is guaranteed to result in a poem, but I'm sure at least a few will spark something.

- Write a poem that starts "If only I'd known... "

- What if you were a superhero or a wizard with magical powers? What would they be? How would you use them?

- Write a poem "On Being _____(write your age here)."

- Write a poem about an animal (real or imaginary) that you would like as a pet (dog, cat, dragon, etc.).

- Respond to a poem you like (or dislike). You can write your poem as a direct answer to the poet or to what the poet is writing about.

- Write a praise poem. This prompt is similar in format to the tribute poem (see page 85), but the subject of the praise poem is YOU! You are the hero. So this is your time to strut your stuff and crow a bit. Consider which metaphors might be appropriate to describe yourself and your life. Consider your heritage, height, color, and nature. Consider the way you "walk in the world."

- Choose a place—your backyard, the floor of your room, the night sky—and mark off a square foot. Write a poem about what you see there. Sometimes it's only by focusing in on the small things that a poet can get at the bigger picture.

- Choose one color and write a poem inspired by it. "Blue Poem," for example, might start with an ink stain, pass by the ocean, and end up at the saddest day of your life.

- Visit your local art museum or gallery. Walk around until you see a painting that really "speaks" to you. Pull out your notebook and freewrite. Describe any people depicted in the painting. Where are they? What are they thinking?

- Write a poem about the animal(s) inside you. Choose one or many. Start off with "The bear in me…" or "The butterfly in me…" or whatever you choose.

- Write a poem from the point of view of your ghost. Where or who would you haunt?

- Write a poem that starts "In my classroom…"

- Like they always say, truth is stranger than fiction. Take a look through your local newspaper and find a story that catches your interest. Use it as a jumping-off point for a poem.

- Write a poem that's all dialogue. Use at least two voices.

- Choose a profession, such as a chef, a doctor, or a painter. Make a long list of verbs that are used in the job. So, for a chef, you might have chop, baste, roast, cook, and so on. Now take this list of verbs and use them to write a poem about something that has nothing to do with the job you chose. I might use my cooking words for a poem about walking in the woods, for instance. This is a great way to get out of a cliché rut.

- Write about a gift.

- Write a poem about packing a suitcase. Let the items you pack tell the story of the traveler, the destination, and the reason for the trip.

- Write a poem from the point of view of somebody very different from yourself. It could be anyone from George Washington to a girl caught in a tornado. It could even be from the perspective of your own parents or teachers. Try to really climb into the mind of that person and see through his or her eyes.

- Write a poem in the form of a tour of your house, school, or other place that you are very familiar with. What particular things are important to point out? Can you shape the way a place is seen by what you choose to show?

- Magical realism is a literary style that gives ordinary objects, people, and situations extraordinary powers. Maybe your computer printer can print out wishes that come true or your blender mixes up love potions. Choose an everyday object and give it some magic in a poem.

- Write a descriptive poem using just one of your senses. Avoid sight. Instead, choose touch, smell, hearing, or taste. Try using a sense that isn't ordinarily used to describe the object. For example, describe the taste of a tree or the sound of cooking dinner.

- Choose a place and write a poem about how it will change over time. Each line might start like this: In 10 years…In 25 years…In 50 years…In 1,000 years…Try the same thing going back in time: 50 years ago…100 years ago…500 years ago…and so on.

- Flip to a page in the dictionary. Blindly point at a word and then challenge yourself to write a poem about that word. Use it as a jumping-off point, then brainstorm and see where you end up.

- Perhaps you've written an "I am" poem. Now, try an "I was" or "I will be" poem.

- Write a poem in the form of a recipe. It can be a recipe for anything: happiness, surviving sixth grade, becoming an outcast … whatever.

- Use the phrase "All right, I may have lied … " to inspire a poem. The phrase can be used as an opener, a closer, or as a refrain throughout. In later drafts the phrase can even be left out altogether. These poems tend to end up having a conversational tone. Remember, poetry does not have to sound stilted and "academic" to be effective.

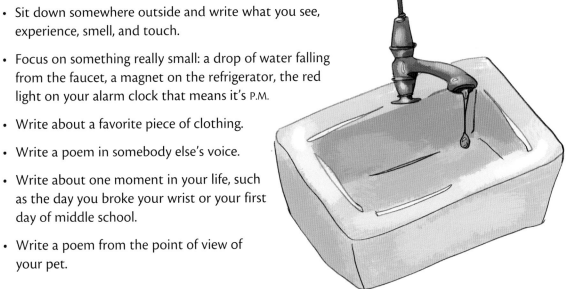

- Sit down somewhere outside and write what you see, experience, smell, and touch.

- Focus on something really small: a drop of water falling from the faucet, a magnet on the refrigerator, the red light on your alarm clock that means it's P.M.

- Write about a favorite piece of clothing.

- Write a poem in somebody else's voice.

- Write about one moment in your life, such as the day you broke your wrist or your first day of middle school.

- Write a poem from the point of view of your pet.

"Ta Da!"
Presenting Your Work

Remember the "secret room" that all poets have in their hearts, the secret room with a view of the world? Well, most poets reach a point when they want to share that special view with others. You might start off by passing your poems to a friend or a family member. Many poets are content to stop there, but if you want to share your writing with a wider range of readers you'll have to consider reading, performing, or publishing your work.

Reading Your Poetry

Keep your eye out for "open mics" taking place at nearby libraries, bookstores, and coffee shops. Some of them are organized specifically for young readers. If no open mic events already exist where you live, you could always help organize one yourself. Many places would welcome a "young people's open mic" as long as someone reliable is willing to organize and run the event (see Hosting a Poetry Bash, page 92).

When reading your work out loud in front of others, be prepared. Determine beforehand which poems you will read and in which order. Print your poems clearly so they're easy to read. Hold the paper or book about shoulder level and slightly to the side. This positions the words close enough so you won't have to bow your head yet not so close that you cover your face. Try looking at your audience occasionally, keeping your place with a thumb or finger. Plant your feet. Speak clearly. Don't rush or mumble.

Sometimes, your poem may require that you give the audience a little background information. ("I wrote this poem after I had a dream in which I go to school and discover that I'm a teacher and all the grown-ups are students!" or "Before I read this poem I should explain that a bandicoot is an Australian marsupial that looks like a cross between a monkey and a squirrel.") Whatever you say, keep your introductory comments to a minimum. If one of your poems cannot "stand on its own" without a lot of explanation, you may want to consider rewriting it, so that its meaning is more apparent (see Accessibility Scale, page 49).

Here are a few other quick reading tips. Do not put down either your poetry or yourself ("This next poem's not very good, but here goes..."). Take a minute to adjust the microphone stand—if there is one—to a comfortable height. Speak directly toward the

microphone—not too close, not too far. Never, ever read longer than you are allotted. Get to know beforehand how much time you'll need to read your poems. Keep a watch with you, and use it! There are others waiting their turn. Lastly, don't leave the event as soon as your turn is over. In the po-biz, this is known as "takin' the mic, then takin' a hike," or "mic 'n' hike" for short. Stay and support your fellow poets; you just may hear something that inspires you.

Someday, you may be lucky enough to have a full-length reading—called a "feature." These can last from 10 minutes to an hour or more. With this added time you should take special care to arrange the order of your poems beforehand. Try to vary the mood and subject matter of the poems you present—a little bit of "ha, ha" and a little bit of "ah ha." And always be prepared to leave out a poem or two if you are in danger of going over your time limit.

Performing Your Poetry

Consider taking your poetry presentation to a new height by memorizing your words and performing them. Poem performance can be a simple matter of telling your poems to your audience much as a storyteller tells a story. Or you can add gestures, movement, and character voices for a more theatrical touch. Either way, what makes poem performance so effective is the act of reciting your words from memory. Because your attention is not focused on a piece of paper or a book, you are free to connect more fully with your audience (see The Secrets of Memorizing Poetry, page 94).

Hosting a Poetry Bash

With a little simple planning, you can host a spoken word event that will offer an opportunity for you and other poets to share your work. If you have access to a coffee shop or a bookstore with a ready-made stage and sound system, then good for you. Otherwise, you have to use your imagination.

You could hold the event in a classroom. No microphone is necessary as long as your audience is small. (Instead of an "open mic" you could call it an "open mouth.")

If you have the time, you can always get more fancy. Any room can be transformed into a poets' café by placing small tables all around, cabaret style. Tablecloths and small votive candles are a nice touch, too. If fire is not allowed, try placing lamps around the room—anything to add a bit of ambience.

Before the show, prepare an open mic sign-up sheet using lined paper. At the top of the paper write this note for all to read:

Only one poem per reader.

Order will be chosen randomly.

If time allows, we'll do another round.

Thanks for sharing your work.

Number each line so your readers write their names in numerical order. If 10 people sign up, place slips of paper numbered from one to 10 into a hat. Now the order can be chosen at random by pulling the numbers out of the hat. This makes the order fair, takes the heat off you, and also provides a bit of fun and suspense as the audience waits to hear who's going to read next.

Insist that every reader share only one poem. That way, everyone has a fair chance. Be sure to save the numbered slips of paper after you read them off, because you may need them again, in case you have time to do another round.

Always begin your poetry bash by thanking everyone for coming and explaining clearly how the event will be run. Encourage the audience to clap as each poet exits the stage area. And, of course, close the show by once again thanking the audience and encouraging everyone to applaud the poets.

I Am Slam; Slam I Am

If you ever have a chance to attend a poetry slam, by all means do! A "slam" is a high-energy poetry performance competition judged by audience members. Individual poems are typically scored by a point system, from one to 10. Chicago construction worker/poet Marc Smith came up with the idea in 1986 to add new luster to otherwise dull poetry readings. Since then, it has grown into a massive international competition.

But be forewarned! At their best, these competitions can be fun and supportive; at their worst, tense and abusive. Some poetry slams are held in venues that don't allow underage poets. Others are more inclusive and welcome young people and teens. I ran a poetry slam for years and remember with satisfaction one competitor who was only eight years old. His 10-year-old brother also competed. The title of the 10-year-old's first poem? "When I was young"! He didn't win the competition, but the audience loved him. When a poetry slam is conducted in the proper spirit, "the points are not the point; the point is poetry," as they say.

The Secrets of Memorizing Poetry

This is a trick title. There are no real secrets as such. You already have the most important memorization tool you'll need—your brain. The word *mnemonics* (nem ON ix), with its silent m, is a fancy way of saying "memorization techniques." You probably already know a few mnemonics—for example, arranging the first letter of each item on a list so that the letters spell a familiar word. Here are a few of my favorite mnemonic devices for memorizing poetry.

Repetition: The Daisy Chain

The more you repeat your poem, the more your reading of it will become second nature with no awkward pauses. What follows is the basic method of memorizing poetry through repetition. I call it the daisy chain method because it requires you to memorize a poem two lines at a time in overlapping pairs, thus connecting the lines like the interlocking links in a chain.

1. Repeat the first line until you can say it 10 times fluently.

2. Then repeat the next line until you can say it 10 times fluently.

3. Then repeat these first two lines together 10 times.

4. Memorize the third line next. Then repeat the second and third lines together. Then the third and fourth lines. Then the fourth and fifth, and so on.

5. Continue memorizing your lines in overlapping pairs so that you're practicing the transition from one line to the next. This will give you experience moving easily from the end of one line to the beginning of the next line.

6. Your final recitation will be more fluid, without those long pauses between lines. Notice that by moving from one pair of overlapping lines to the next, you avoid continually starting over at the beginning of the poem, a mistake that puts too much emphasis on the first half of the poem and deprives the second half.

7. After you've made it through the entire poem working with the overlapping pairs, go back and attempt to recite four lines at a time, then six lines, thus increasing the size of your groupings until eventually you can recite the entire poem.

Rememberization

As a rule of thumb, the best way to truly internalize a poem is to memorize it over the course of many days. It's better to devote 20 minutes per day over five days—a total of one hour, 40 minutes—than to devote a total of four hours in one night. Just as important as the time spent memorizing is the time between memorization sessions. It's on the second day of memorization that a phenomenon I call *rememberization* begins.

On your second day of memorization, you have the additional task of *remembering* what you've memorized—thus the term *rememberization*. If memorization is the process of adding a poem to your *short-term* memory, then rememberization is the process of adding the poem to your *long-term* memory. If you're like most people, you can memorize a typical eight-line poem with a couple hours of concentrated effort. But then the next day you might not be able to recite a single word! Don't be discouraged. This lapse is actually a good thing and part of the natural process of committing poetry to memory.

It helps if you think of your short-term memory as a pit of quicksand. The poem you placed there yesterday has been sucked under the surface. The next day your task is to reach into the pit and bring the poem back up! The day after that, the poem may be gone again. And again you must roll up your sleeve and rescue your poem from the depths. Do this every day and eventually you'll be able to retrieve your poem quickly without hesitation.

Other Tips for Memorizing Poetry

- **Relax:** memorization is a lot easier when you're relaxed.

- **Get rid of background noise:** it's difficult to memorize with the radio or TV on.

- **Combine techniques:** use a combination of memorization techniques—listening to the poem, saying the poem, writing the poem, reading the poem, acting it out, setting it to music, dancing to it, etc.

- **Memorize a poem you like:** it's typically easier to memorize a poem that you like. On the other hand, if you're required to memorize a poem you don't initially like, you may grow to appreciate it more as you memorize it.

- **Memorize while standing up:** typically, you won't be reciting poetry while seated. It's always best to involve your whole body in the memorization process, if possible.

- **Create memorization movements:** for each word or cluster of words in the poem, create a body movement that will help you remember what comes next. Many people can remember movements more easily than words.

- **Speak out:** speak your poems out loud as you repeat the lines. This gives you experience listening to your own voice and, again, gets your body involved.

- **Memorize multiple poems together:** if your goal is to memorize more than one poem, you're best off dividing your time between them each day. Don't wait until you've finished one before starting on the next.

- **Use a tape recorder:** if possible, record your poem using a hand-held tape recorder. Listen to it repeatedly. Gradually begin to recite along. Think how many songs you've memorized like this already, simply by hearing them on the radio or in your earphones.

- **Memorize the last part first:** for especially long poems, try memorizing the last half first. We tend to repeat the first part of the poem more when memorizing it, and so we learn the first part better. It's good to know both halves of a long poem equally well, but if you have to choose, it's better to start shaky and finish smooth. Also, for some reason, memorizing the first half always seems easier when you've already got the second half down. That way, all you have to do is meet yourself in the middle!

- **Create your own mnemonics:** conjure up your own pictures, initials, phrases, associations, and movements—anything to help you remember what word comes next.

- **Speed-through rehearse:** if you have successfully memorized your poem, but your recitation is still tentative and halting, try saying the words as quickly as you can with little to no expression. The idea is to learn the transitions from line to line and from stanza to stanza so you don't stop the flow of your reading. I like to line up 10 M&Ms and eat my way through them as I complete each recitation. If you can complete 10 speed-throughs of your poem, you are probably ready to recite it in front of a live audience.

Get Published!

For most of us writers, there's nothing quite like the satisfaction of seeing our own words in print. Young poets have many publishing options.

1. Think Local

Your school may have a literary magazine or include poems in a school newspaper. If your school prints a yearbook, approach those in charge about including poetry. Sometimes the local newspaper will print poetry submissions. It's worth a try.

2. Go National

Once you have explored all your local publishing opportunities, try submitting your work to one of the many national publications that feature young writers. Start with the list

of literary reference books, magazines, and Web sites provided at the back of this book (see Publishing Resources for Young Poets, page 111). This list includes a few of the most long-lived and reliable sources. You will no doubt find more as you explore.

It's a good policy never to submit your poetry to an organization that expects you to pay a submission fee or pay to receive a copy of the publication if your poem is accepted. Few legitimate magazine publishers pay money, but they will at least send you two or more copies as payment if they accept your poem. Literary magazines that publish poetry by adults will sometimes require a reading fee as a way of paying for the cost of publication. If you're a young poet, your time is best spent submitting your work to publications designed for or by other young writers.

3. Seek a Publisher?

It's difficult (nearly impossible) for adult poets to get a full-length book of poems printed by a major publisher. As a young poet, the odds are even worse. Most major publishers won't consider your manuscript until you have an established publishing record with literary magazines or some other "hook" that would assure your book will sell.

Do It Yourself

Many poets, young and old, emerging and established, have turned to self-publishing. A *chapbook* is easy to make and provides poets with something to give to friends or to sell at readings. Here are a bunch of different books you can put together. Play with sizes, shapes, colored paper, whatever.

SEW EASY

This easy-to-make book is sewn together with a simple stitch. This book measures $4^1/_2$ x $5^3/_4$ inches, but you can make yours whatever size you want. Just make sure your cover is a little bit bigger than the paper you want to put inside it.

WHAT YOU NEED

- 3 pieces of $8^1/_2$ x 11-inch paper
- Scissors
- 1 piece of card stock, $5^3/_4$ x 9 inches
- Ruler
- Pencil
- Needle
- Waxed linen* or dental floss
- Glue (optional)
- Design materials to decorate the front cover
  *Available at bead shops and craft stores

WHAT YOU DO

1. Fold each piece of the $8^1/_2$ x 11-inch paper in half to create six pieces measuring $5^1/_2$ x $8^1/_2$ inches. Cut them in half with scissors.

2. Fold each of the pages carefully in half. Each folded page will now be $4^1/_4$ x $5^1/_2$ inches. Stack the pages together.

3. Fold the card stock in half. This is now the cover of your book. Place the folded pages inside the cover, centering them in the fold.

4. Using the ruler and pencil, carefully mark three holes at the fold. Space the holes evenly, making one at the center of the fold and the others on either side of the first, about $1^1/_2$ inches away. With the needle, pierce through all six folded papers and the cover.

5. Thread the needle with a piece of waxed linen or dental floss about 18 inches long.

6. From the outside, bring the needle into the center of the book through the middle hole. Take the needle back out at the top hole. Come back to the inside at the bottom hole. Finally, go out again at the center hole (figure 1). Unthread the needle and set it aside.

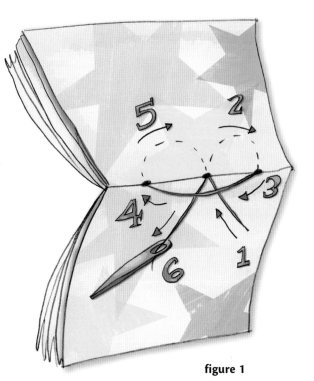

figure 1

7. Turn the book over and look at the outside. You'll see the thread running along the spine from the top to bottom holes, and two tails of thread hanging from the center hole. Arrange the tails so that there is one on each side of the long stitch running along the side. Tie the thread tails in a knot. Write or glue your poems into the book. Decorate the cover and inside pages however you want.

BIND 'EM UP

Here are four bindings you can do in no time at all. All you need are your printed poems and a few supplies. Play with different sizes and shapes if you want.

Staples and Tape Binding

1. Gather all the pages of your manuscript together and line up their edges. Hold the pages in place with paper clips. Measure and mark two pieces of colored paper $1/4$ inch larger on all four sides than the pages. Cut out the pieces.

2. Write or type the title and your name on the cover. Center the front cover on top of the pages. Center the bottom cover under the pages. Staple down along the spine of the book about $1/2$ inch from the edge. Press a piece of cloth adhesive tape over the bound edge, covering the staples.

Binder Ring Binding

1. Create three holes on the left-hand side of the manuscript. See step 1 from the Brass Fastener instructions. Thread individual binder rings through the three holes. You can find binder rings at craft and office supply stores.

Simple Sewn Binding

1. Follow step 1 from the Brass Fastener instructions.

2. Pass the yarn down through the center hole. Then pass it up through the top hole. Pass it down through the bottom hole. Then sew up through the center hole. Pull the thread ends tight, then tie the ends together over the long top thread. Tie a knot or bow.

Brass Fastener Binding

1. Use a three-hole punch to create the holes on the left-hand side of the manuscript. If you don't have a three-hole punch, mark the holes for the fasteners by placing a sheet of loose-leaf paper on top of the front cover with the holes at the left side, leaving the $1/4$-inch border around the other three sides. Mark the hole positions with the pencil and use a nail to create the holes.

2. Push the brass fasteners through the holes from the front cover through the pages and the back cover, then spread apart the fasteners' legs so they lie flat.

Start a Writer's Group

One of the best ways to get strong, positive feedback on your writing is to start a writer's group/workshop with friends who are also interested in writing. Simply speaking, a writer's group meets once or twice a month for members to share their thoughts on each other's writing and to offer encouragement, ideas, and advice on becoming more effective writers. In a writing group, everyone gets an equal chance to have his or her work shared.

What You'll Get Out of a Writer's Group

- By reading your writing to others and receiving feedback from them, you'll be better prepared for submitting your work for publication.

- You'll have the opportunity to discuss the strong points of your writing, as well as the parts that need work.

- You may make some new friends who also like to write.

- You get to eat snacks.

How to Get People Interested

- Post a notice about your new writer's group on the bulletin boards at school or at a local bookstore or community center.

- Email friends, classmates, cousins, or anyone else around the same age as you that might be interested.

What You Need to Establish Before the First Meeting

- When you'll meet: Make sure it is a convenient time for the whole group. Try to meet at least once a month.

- Where you'll meet: An empty classroom after school works well (ask a teacher first), or meet at someone's home in a room with no family traffic during meeting time.

- How long each meeting will last: The meeting should be long enough for each member to have a chance to read his or her work and receive feedback.

- How many members there'll be: If you have more than five to seven members, you may not have enough time to read and comment on each person's work.

- Who'll bring snacks: Snacks are an important part of meeting together. Develop a list of who'll bring what.

The First Meeting

- Have members bring one piece of writing they want to read, with enough copies for the rest of the group.

- Have the group members pass out their writing, and explain that each member should read them and write comments before the next meeting.

- It may be a good idea for members to introduce themselves to the group, stating what their goals are while in the group, what kind of writing they like, what their favorite books are, and so on.

Workshop Rules

- At the next meeting, the first reader should read his or her work, while the others read along silently.

- Go around the room and have each member comment on the piece. Have them first start off with something positive about the piece. It's also important that no one in the group makes fun of somebody and/or her writing. Nobody wants to share in an unfriendly environment.

- The writer should not speak while the comments are going on.

- Make sure someone is keeping track of the time so that everyone will have a chance.

- After all the comments are heard, each member should hand the marked-up copy of the piece of writing to the reader. Then the next person reads,.

- After several meetings, you can suggest starting up a newsletter featuring the writing from the group.

Questions to Ask Yourself While Reading Someone's Work:

- What works for you? Why?
- What doesn't work for you? Why not?
- Which parts confuse you?
- What sounds interesting to you?
- What would you like to read more about?
- What supportive comments can I add?
- What ideas do I have regarding this piece?

A Promise. A Warning. A Final Word of Hope.

The best publishing advice I've ever heard comes from an unlikely source, the inventor Thomas Alva Edison. Edison said, "Genius is one percent inspiration and ninety-nine percent perspiration. Accordingly, a 'genius' is often merely a talented person who has done all of his or her homework." I promise you that if you have the talent and the patience and you "do your homework," you will eventually see your writing in print. You will be thrilled when the work is accepted and fulfilled when the work is published.

But here's a word of warning from a poet who knows: most professional writers do not ever become rich. Most of us work really hard to establish a career and gradually, over time, we make a humble living. I was in my 40s and had published my sixth book before I was able to quit a part-time job delivering newspapers. Perhaps your story will be different. Perhaps your poetry will earn you great riches and fame. Perhaps you will live like the king or the queen in the poem that opens this book. But if not, you'll have to be content with the many other rewards of living the poet's life.

Better to live a poet's life than the life of kings and queens. I've been living the poet's life since I was about 12. My career as a writer of books happened as a secondary result of my love of writing poetry. The novelty of publication wears off. The money comes and goes. But nothing can alter the simple magic of the bloom, and the boom, and the secret room.

We poets are driven by the simple need to express ourselves. To make sense of our world and the feelings we feel and to somehow capture it all in a poem. To discover the blooms with our eyes, to create the booms in our minds, all the while looking out on the world from the secret rooms in our hearts— that place where nearly all poems start.

Appendix A:
Selected Poems

Here is a list of poems that are worth getting to know. Some are classics; some are popular; some are just plain fun. You can find them at your library or bookstore, of course. In many cases, you can also do an Internet search. Many living poets have websites. Classic poets may have several web pages devoted to their works.

"Because I Could Not Stop for Death" by Emily Dickinson

"The Blind Men and the Elephant" by John Godfrey Saxe

"Brown Penny" by William Butler Yeats

"Casey at the Bat" by Ernest Lawrence Thayer

"Constantly Risking Absurdity" by Lawrence Ferlinghetti

"The Cremation of Sam McGee" by Robert W. Service

"Daffodils" by William Wordsworth

"Fifteen" by William Stafford

"The Fish" by Elizabeth Bishop

"Fog" by Carl Sandburg

"From Clearances-3" by Seamus Heaney

"Harlem" by Langston Hughes

"The Highwayman" by Alfred Noyes

"Hippopotamus" by Joanna Cole

"How Do I Love Thee" by Elizabeth Barrett Browning

"The Human Family" by Countee Cullen

"If" by Rudyard Kipling

"in just spring" by E. E. Cummings

"Introduction to Songs of Innocence" by William Blake

"Invitation" by Shel Silverstein

"I Wandered Lonely as a Cloud" by William Wordsworth

"Jabberwocky" by Lewis Carroll

"Life Is Fine" by Langston Hughes

"Little Orphant Annie" by James Whitcomb Riley

"Maybe Dats Youwr Pwoblem Too" by Jim Hall

"Mending Wall" by Robert Frost

"Metaphor" by Eve Merriam

"Miracles" by Walt Whitman

"My Papa's Waltz" by Theodore Roethke

"The New Kid on the Block" by Jack Prelutsky

"next to of course god america i" by E. E. Cummings

Selected Poems (continued)

"Ozymandias" by Percy Bysshe Shelley

"Paul Revere's Ride"
by Henry Wadsworth Longfellow

"Preposterous" by Jim Hall

"Phenomenal Woman" by Maya Angelou

"The Raven" by Edgar Allan Poe

"The Red Wheelbarrow"
by William Carlos Williams

"Reply to the Question: 'How Can You
Become a Poet?'" by Eve Merriam

"Richard Cory"
by Edwin Arlington Robinson

"Road Not Taken" by Robert Frost

"The Second Coming"
by William Butler Yeats

"Shall I Compare Thee to a Summer's Day
(Sonnet 18)" by William Shakespeare

"Sick" by Shel Silverstein

"Solitude" by Ella Wheeler Wilcox

"Stopping by Woods on a Snowy Evening"
by Robert Frost

"Sympathy" by Paul Laurence Dunbar

"The Tiger" by William Blake

"A Visit from Saint Nicholas"
by Clement C. Moore

"The Waking" by Theodore Roethke

"We Real Cool" by Gwendolyn Brooks

"Wynken, Blynken and Nod"
by Eugene Field

Appendix B:
Selected Poets

These poets are challenging and yet "accessible." In other words, they don't leave you scratching your head and looking cross-eyed. An * indicates that the poet writes specifically for older kids and young adults.

Maya Angelou
Gwendolyn Brooks
Deborah Chandra*
Billy Collins
Emily Dickinson
Robert Frost
Kristine O'Connell George*
Charles Ghigna
Nikki Giovanni
Nikki Grimes
Georgia Heard
Betsy Hearne
Sara Holbrook*
Lee Bennett Hopkins
Langston Hughes
Paul B. Janeczko
Ted Kooser
J. Patrick Lewis
Walter Dean Myers*
Marilyn Nelson
Naomi Shihab Nye
Mary Oliver
Liz Rosenberg
Carl Sandburg
Jon Sciezcka
Sonya Sones
Gary Soto
William Stafford
Wislawa Szymborska
Maria Testa

Publishing Resources for Young Poets

Looking for a place to submit your poems? Here's a short list of possibilities. Never submit your work to a magazine or website you haven't read. And never submit your work until you have read the publisher's submission guidelines. When sending submissions to any magazine, include a self-addressed, stamped envelope if you expect a reply.

Cicada Magazine and *Cricket Magazine*
www.cricketmag.com
Carus Publishing Company
315 Fifth St., P.O. Box 300, Peru, IL 61354

Creative Kids Magazine: The National Voice for Kids
www.prufrock.com
Submissions Editor, P.O. Box 8813
Waco, TX 76714-8813
Email: ck@prufrock.com

New Library of Young Adult Writing
www.merlynspen.com

New Moon: The Magazine for Girls and Their Dreams
www.newmoonmagazine.org
2 W First Street, #101, Duluth MN 55802
Email: girl@newmoon.org

Poets & Writers, Inc.
www.pw.org

Potato Hill Poetry
www.potatohill.com
6 Peasant Street, Suite #2, South Natick, MA 01760
Email: info@potatohill.com

Skipping Stones Magazine
www.skippingstones.org
P.O. Box 3939, Eugene, OR 97403
Email: Editor@SkippingStones.org

Stone Soup: The Magazine By Young Writers and Artists
www.stonesoup.com
Submissions Department, Box 83
Santa Cruz, CA 95063
Email: editor@stonesoup.com

Teen Ink
www.teenink.com
Box 30, Newton, MA 02461
Email: submissions@teenlink.com

Teen Voices (girls only)
www.teenvoices.com
P.O. Box 120027, Boston, MA 02112-0027

Upwords Poetry
www.upwordspoetry.com

What If? Magazine (Canada only)
www.whatifmagazine.com
19 Lynwood Place, Guelph, Ontario N1G 2V9
Email: poetry@whatifmagazine.com

Other Useful Resources

The Poet's Market (Writers Digest Books). This reference book comes out in a new edition every year. It's a fantastic resource for any serious poet, full of contact info and submissions guidelines for the "grown up" poetry publications.

The Young Writer's Guide to Getting Published (Writers Digest Books, 2001) by Kathy Henderson. This, sixth edition, replaces the earlier *Market Guide for Young Writers: Where and How to Sell What You Write*. Check to be sure you get the most updated edition.

A Teen's Guide to Getting Published (Prufrock Press, 1996) by Danielle and Jessica Dunn. Written by teens for teens.

So, You Wanna be a Writer? How to Get Published and Maybe Even Make it Big! (Beyond Words Publishing, 2001) by Vicki Hambleton and Cathleen Greenwood.

Glossary

accent. Reading a poem as if you are from a different country. (Ha ha.)

accessibility. How easy or difficult a poem is to understand.

alliteration. Typically defined as the repetition of consonant sounds at the beginning of successive words. (I'd like to linger a little longer but it's getting a little late.) Note: Fully defined, alliteration encompasses repetition of both consonant sounds AND vowel sounds. Consonance (repetition of consonant sounds) and assonance (repetition of vowel sounds) are, truly, both forms of alliteration.

anthropomorphism. The act of human beings reading their own feelings into nonhuman objects or beings.

assonance. The repetition of vowel sounds. (The Eskimo's only hope.) *Also see* alliteration.

beat. Roughly equivalent to the number of feet in a poetic line. Along with meter, beat helps establish a poem's distinctive rhythm.

bent book. Small notebook carried by po-folk.

chapbook. A small book containing poems.

closed form. Any of a variety of poetry forms with a prescribed structure.

consonance. The repetition of consonant sounds usually within or at the end of successive words. (Mike Brunk stacked the cooked steaks. Shadow-meadow. Pressed-passed.) *Also see* alliteration.

couplet. Two lines of verse, usually rhymed. ("I think that I shall never see / A poem as lovely as a tree." —Joyce Kilmer.)

didactic poetry. Poetry that contains a moral or teaches a lesson; poetry with a "message."

enjambed line. See run-on line.

epic. A very long poem that typically tells an involved heroic story. (Homer's *Odyssey*.)

foot. Metrical unit of measure roughly equivalent to the beat of a poetic line.

form. The shape of a poem.

free verse. Poetry with no prescribed structure.

ink hemorrhage. When your ink pen bursts in your pocket and ruins your pants.

irony. A situation or statement involving some sort of incongruity or discrepancy.

lyric. As opposed to narrative and dramatic poetry, the lyric retains the poetic elements typically associated with musical expression: singing, chanting, or reciting to musical accompaniment. In these modern times, the distinctions among lyric, narrative, and dramatic poetry are not so relevant.

media madness. Lessened creativity due to too much passive contact with media.

metaphor. A figure of speech in which something is spoken of in terms of something else for the value of comparison (i.e., love is a "shy flower," the fog sits "on silent haunches"). Simile is a type of metaphorical language. *See* simile.

meter. Literally the measure of a poetic line.

mic 'n' hike. Leaving an open mic immediately after you read.

mnemonic. A trick used to remember something.

mood. The feeling elicited by a poem (e.g., sad, merry, whimsical, frightening, supernatural, frantic, etc.).

narrative poem. A poem that tells a story. Long narrative poetry can be divided into four stages: introduction, development, climax, and resolution. ("Casey at the Bat" by Ernest Lawrence Thayer.)

no-po. A non-poetry person.

ode. Simply defined, an ode is a formalized poem in which the poet addresses the poem's subject directly. Odes are typically rhymed and use heightened language.

onomatopoeia. The use of words that sound like the action, thing, or person they represent (i.e., crash, hammer, click, boom, sweeper).

open form. Lack of prescribed structure or rhyme scheme as in free verse.

open mic. A public forum in which poets share their work.

page fright. Fear of beginning a new poem.

performance poetry. Poems that are presented to an audience in an expressive, theatrical way, often from memory. The distinction between performance poetry and other "types" of poetry is often arbitrary.

personification. The act of giving human qualities to nonhuman things ("the trees whispered") and abstractions ("love took a holiday"). *See* anthropomorphism.

po-folk. People who really like poetry.

po-biz. The "business" of practicing the craft and profession of poetry.

refrain. A word, phrase, or line that is repeated throughout a poem. ("I must go down to the seas again" from John Masefield's "Sea Fever.")

rhythm. The flow of syllables across the steady structure established by the meter and beat of a poem; the poem's "groove."

run-on line. Poetic line that does not end in accordance with any natural pause in speech, but rather carries over to the succeeding line.

sibilance. Hissing sound, as in "seashells for sale."

simile. A figure of speech in which something is said to be like something else (i.e., "love is like a shy flower," "feeling fit as a fiddle," "eyes black as night," "sweeter than honey"). The comparison is usually between two unlike things and typically involves the words like, as, such as, or than.

slam. A spirited performance poetry competition judged by the audience.

stanza. A poetic paragraph.

Selected Bibliography

Chandra, Deborah. *Rich Lizard and Other Poems.* New York: Farrar Straus Giroux, 1993.

Cisneros, Sandra. *House on Mango Street.* New York: Vintage Books, 1989.

Creech, Sharon. *Love That Dog.* New York: Scholastic Inc., 2001.

Fleischman, Paul. *Joyful Noise: Poems for Two Voices.* New York: HarperCollins Publishers/Charlotte Zolotow, 1988.

Fletcher, Ralph. *A Writer's Notebook: Unlocking the Writer Within You.* New York: Harper Trophy, 1996.

Fletcher, Ralph. *Writing a Poem from the Inside Out.* New York: Harper Trophy, 2002.

George, Kristine O'Connell. *Swimming Upstream: Middle School Poems.* New York: Clarion Books, 2002.

Ghigna, Charles. *A Fury of Motion: Poems for Boys.* Honesdale, PA: Boyds Mill Press, 2003.

Glaser, Isabel Joshlin. *Dreams of Glory: Poems Starring Girls.* New York: Atheneum Books for Young Readers, 1995.

Goldstein, Bobbye S. *Inner Chimes: Poems on Poetry.* Honesdale, PA.: Wordsong/Boyds Mills Press, 1992.

Gordon, Ruth, ed. *Pierced by a Ray of Sun: Poems About Times We Feel Alone.* New York: HarperCollins Publishers, 1995.

Heard, Georgia, ed. *This Place I Know: Poems of Comfort.* Cambridge, MA: Candlewick Press, 2002.

Holbrook, Sara. *I Never Said I Wasn't Difficult and Other Poems.* Honesdale, PA: Wordsong/Boyds Mills Press, 1999.

_____. *Walking on the Boundaries of Change: Poems of Transition.* Honesdale, PA: Wordsong/Boyds Mills Press, 2000.

_____. *Wham! It's a Poetry Jam: Discovering Performance Poetry.* Honesdale, PA: Wordsong/Boyds Mills Press, 2002.

Janeczko, Paul B., ed. *A Kick in the Head: A Young Person's Guide to Poetic Forms.* Cambridge, MA.: Candlewick Press, 2005.

_____, ed. *A Poke in the I: A Collection of Concrete Poems.* Cambridge, MA: Candlewick Press, 2001.

_____, ed. *The Place My Words Are Looking For: What Poets Say About and Through Their Work.* New York: Bradbury Press, 1990.

Hopkins, Lee Bennett. *Been to Yesterdays: Poems of a Life.* Honesdale, PA: Wordsong/Boyds Mill Press, 1995.

Koch, Kenneth, and Kate Farrell, eds. *Talking to the Sun: An Illustrated Anthology of Poems for Young People.* New York: The Metropolitan Museum of Art/Henry Holt and Company, 1985.

Lane, Barry. *After the End: Teaching and Learning Creative Revision.* Portsmouth, NH: Heinemann, 1992.

Lyne, Sandford, ed. *Ten-Second Rainshowers: Poems by Young People.* New York: Simon & Schuster Books for Young Readers, 1996.

Lyon, George Ella. *Where I'm From, Where Poems Come From.* Spring, TX: Absey & Co., Inc., 1999.

Miller, E. Ethlebert, ed. *In Search of Color Everywhere: A Collection of African-American Poetry.* New York: Stewart, Tabori & Chang, 1994.

Morrison, Lillian. *Rhythm Road: Poems to Move To.* New York: Lothrop, Lee & Shepard Books, 1988.

Panzer, Nora, ed. *Celebrate America in Poetry and Art.* New York: Hyperion Books for Children, 1994.

Rosen, Michael. *Classic Poetry: An Illustrated Collection.* Cambridge, MA.: Candlewick Press, 1998.

Rosenberg, Liz, ed. *The Invisible Ladder: An Anthology of Contemporary American Poems for Young Readers.* New York: Henry Holt and Company, 1996.

Credits

Every effort has been made to trace the ownership of all copyrighted material and to secure the necessary permission to reprint these selections. In the event of any question arising as to the use of any material, the editor and publisher, while expressing regret for any inadvertent error, will be happy to make the necessary correction in future printings. Grateful acknowledgment is made to the following for permission to reprint the copyrighted materials listed below.

Acknowledgments

For 13 years I co-directed the Poetry Alive! Summer Residency Institute for Teachers with Cheryl Bromley Jones. Many of the writing prompts included in this book and much of my educational philosophy springs wholly or in part from my long-time collaboration with this master teacher and true friend.

Thanks also to: Lark editor, Joe Rhatigan, for suggesting this book and for his huge effort to create clear order from chaos; Nathalie Mornu for all the tedious permissions work; Celia Naranjo for her wonderful design work; and Tuesday Mourning for her awesome illustrations.

For support, ideas, advice, and friendship, thanks to Janet Allen, Charles Ghigna, Lee Bennett Hopkins, Paul Janeczko, Alice Naylor, Edie Moon, Bob Falls, Glenis Redmond, and Jon Sarver. Thanks also to all the poets who allowed their words to be a part of this book. And of course, big thanks go to the hundreds of teachers and thousands of young people who have immersed themselves in verse with me over the years leading up to this book.